8/00

ALSO BY HENRY GRUNWALD

*One Man's America: A Journalist's Search
for the Heart of His Country*

TWILIGHT

TWILIGHT

LOSING SIGHT, GAINING INSIGHT

Henry Grunwald

ALFRED A. KNOPF

NEW YORK

1999

THIS IS A BORZOI BOOK
PUBLISHED BY ALFRED A. KNOPF, INC.

Copyright © 1999 by Henry Grunwald

All rights reserved under International and Pan-American Copyright
Conventions. Published in the United States by Alfred A. Knopf,
Inc., New York, and simultaneously in Canada by Random House
of Canada Limited, Toronto. Distributed by Random House, Inc.,
New York.

www.randomhouse.com

Knopf, Borzoi Books, and the colophon are registered
trademarks of Random House, Inc.

Portions of the poem "Quintet for 4½ Senses, Macular Degeneration:
A Progress Report" from the unpublished collection *The Eye Inside the
Storm* are reprinted here by permission of the author, Marilyn Jurich.

Library of Congress Cataloging-in-Publication Data
Grunwald, Henry A. (Henry Anatole)
    Twilight : losing sight, gaining insight / Henry Grunwald.
        p.   cm.
    ISBN 0-375-40422-8
    1. Grunwald, Henry A. (Henry Anatole)   2. Retinal
degeneration—Patients—United States Biography.   3. Blind aged—
United States Biography.   4. Editors—United States Biography.
I. Title.
PN4874.G79A3   1999
362.4'1'092—dc21
[B]   99-35757
                                                             CIP

Manufactured in the United States of America
Published November 3, 1999
Second Printing, December 1999

For Meta
In loving memory

ACKNOWLEDGMENTS

The severe eye problem I describe in this book made me more than ever dependent on the help of my collaborator, Sarah Lewis, who not only took down my words and tirelessly read them back to me but also functioned as an invaluable editor, critic, researcher, and source of inspiration. My gratitude to her is boundless.

My assistant, Dorothy Paulsen, had to carry many extra burdens while I was writing this book. She was cheerful and inexhaustible in keeping my office and much of my life in order.

My wife, Louise, followed successive versions of the manuscript, always ready with encouragement and creative suggestions. She read to me continually from newspapers, magazines, and books. Her keen eyes supplemented, and sometimes substituted for, my own limited vision. She described and explained people and places, landscapes and architecture; and, with her knowledge of art, she brought paintings and sculpture to life for me. For all this and more she has my loving thanks.

My children—Peter, Mandy, and Lisa—helped me as a writer with good advice as well as vivid recollections, and helped me as their father with close and affectionate support.

My doctors David Guyer and Lawrence Yannuzzi not only treated me with skill and devotion but tutored me in the intricacies of macular degeneration and eye problems in general.

I gained much information and practical help from many members of that splendid institution the Lighthouse in New York, including its president, Barbara Silverstone; one of its guiding spirits, Dr. Eleanor Eaton Faye; and the low vision expert Dr. Bruce Rosenthal. A special source of inspiration was Dr. Josephine DeFini.

Nikolai Stevenson, the founder and head of the Association for Macular Diseases, gave me his friendship and wise perspective on our ailment, and an example of how to accept it with patience and good humor.

I am indebted for research help to Stephen Mihm of the *New York Times Magazine;* Brigid O'Hara-Forster of *Time-Europe* in London; Edmund McMahon Turner of Moorfields Hospi-

Acknowledgments

tal, London; John Handley of the American Academy of Ophthalmology; Professor Robert Gurland of New York University; James Cassetta of the Pearl River, New York, Public Library; and the *Time* Research Services.

I am grateful for guidance in the arts to Everett Fahy of the New York Metropolitan Museum of Art, the late designer Mark Hampton, the author and musicologist Jonathan Schwartz, and Mandy Patinkin.

My thanks also to my very constructive editor, Dan Frank; to Harold Evans for his initial support of this project; and to my friend and agent, Lynn Nesbit of Janklow and Nesbit, for her enthusiastic backing.

The New Yorker, under the editorship of Tina Brown, published an article in 1996 called "Losing Sight," which was the starting point for this book.

TWILIGHT

1

In the primordial ocean, a tiny organism stirs. It is covered with a light-sensitive pigment, an eye-spot, that seeks the sun and turns the organism toward it. The act is not seeing, but the precursor of seeing. It is part of the fundamental impulse in all living things to reach for light, part of the indomitable will to see.

I stand at the edge of the ocean and I think of those eyespots and of the single-cell creatures that, eons ago, began the miraculous process of sight. I, too, strain to see—to see the waves, the sand, the shells and seaweed and debris that wash ashore. My eyes are animated by the same impulse, the same will to see. But my eyes don't work, at least not fully, because they are blocked by disease. The scene around me appears through a kind of curtain, a haze. If I bend down, I will have a hard time telling a stone apart from a shell, a coin from a piece of sea glass. If I were to pick up a discarded newspaper, I would not be able to read it. During a lifetime as a writer and editor, reading newspapers—or news in any form—had been a natural and indispensable part of myself. My existence seemed to be wrapped in the printed word. No longer.

Until the onset of my disease, I was literally unaware of my eyes, with the occasional trivial exception of needing new glasses or having some-body extricate a speck of dust. Now I am aware of my eyes almost constantly. I imagine them as dis-tinct globes inside my head. I try to visualize the intricate vessels and veins and conduits in these globes. I think of their fragility but also of their power. In medicine as well as in romantic poetry, it is the heart that is the center and controlling mechanism of life. If the heart stops, life stops. The loss of sight does not mean death. Yet for ages, the eye was believed to contain a human being's vital essence—a not wholly irrational belief. For those of us who are born with the abil-ity to see, sight determines most of what we know about the world, what we enjoy, and what and whom we love. That is surely one reason why in the mythology of almost every culture the eye plays a dominant part.

My years with failing vision have prompted

me to learn about the nature of the eye and the incredible gift of sight, which I had always taken for granted until it began to slip away. But I also learned about living within limits and overcoming disability. This, then, is not merely a story about seeing but also about living. It is a story not merely about losing sight but about gaining insight as well.

In 1992, my wife, Louise, and I rented a villa outside Florence. The light in the house was inadequate, especially in the gloomy, rainy weather of that October; the twenty-five-watt bulbs in the pseudoelegant sconces reminded me of those notoriously underlit Russian hotel rooms. One afternoon, I picked up a carafe from a side table in a particularly dark corner to pour water into a glass. I missed the glass. I inveighed against the landlord, who, I thought, was trying to save electricity with those weak lightbulbs, but I suspected that I might need new glasses. Back in New York, quite unconcerned, I dropped in on the nearest optician. In a darkened cubicle, he took me through the usual eye test. I have worn glasses ever since I was a teenager. Using both eyes, I read the chart without difficulty, but when my right eye was covered and I looked only through the left, I saw virtually nothing. My right eye, on the other hand, was close to normal and, as I realized later, saw for both. The optician seemed embarrassed, and he took me through the test again. The result was the same. "I think you had better see an eye doctor," he said.

Still not too alarmed, I did just that and was told that I was suffering from something called macular degeneration. I did not know what macular meant, but I soon learned that the word derives from *macula* (Latin for "spot") and refers to a tiny area in the retina. As for *degeneration* the term was extremely depressing, with its overtones of moral decay. I had never heard of the disease.

It is formally known as age-related macular degeneration, or AMD, because most sufferers are over fifty. It is one of the least understood eye problems, not having been reliably identified until the 1970s. To one degree or another, it afflicts an estimated 15 million Americans and will beset millions more in the future. It is the most common cause of irreversible vision loss in the world, yet its origins are unknown.

No incident like the missed water glass in Florence occurred again, but I started to look for the leading experts, asking doctors and friends if they could suggest anyone. I found that there were not too many specialists in the field. From among several recommended, I chose a busy Manhattan group of seven doctors with the formidable name of Vitreous-Retina-Macular Consultants of New York. In the crowded waiting room I observed the other patients. Some seemed perfectly normal, while others moved unsteadily, a few using walking sticks, some guided by relatives or nurses. I began to sense a kind of hierarchy of illness and, to my shame, could not suppress a slight feeling of superiority over those who were worse off than I.

The doctors who took me in hand were Lawrence Yannuzzi and David Guyer. They examined my eyes through the familiar machine (known as a Haag-Streit slit-lamp biomicroscope) with its pair of lenses in the center of two large black disks that looked like eyes belonging to a robot. They performed another examination, called a fluorescein angiogram, which involved the injection of a dye into the veins. I was warned that it causes a brief wave of nausea in some patients. It did, but I was told to breathe deeply, and the feeling passed. The dye travels through the body, including the eye, and any changes that have occurred in the retina can then be recorded by a special camera in a series of photographs. These are accompanied by bursts of light, as startling and disorienting as if a flashbulb had gone off immediately in front of one's eyes. I saw the resulting pictures on a computer screen and later in glossy prints. They showed a large reddish circle shot through with odd-shaped streaks and splotches. I imagined that it was the map of a strange planet. Explanations followed. Guyer was energetic but quiet, studious-looking, and with a contained passion for his specialty. Yannuzzi was equally passionate, but more kinetic, and positively sprayed scientific knowledge. He told me later that he had been drawn to ophthalmology partly because it was "like reading Sherlock Holmes, like solving a mystery."

Guyer and Yannuzzi began to induct me into the mysteries of macular degeneration and, more generally, of how the eye works. I have always been amused by our habit of comparing human organs to machines—"The heart is a pump"—as if nature were copying technology, rather than the other way around. So I had to smile when Dr. Guyer said, "The eye is a camera." The clear front of the eye, consisting of cornea, pupil, and lens, lets in light and focuses it on the back of the eye. The back is covered by a thin layer of tissue, the retina, which acts like the film in a camera. The retina was described as a sort of "seeing tissue," and that startled me in its mysteriousness; how could tissue "see"? The retina, I learned, consists of light-sensitive cones and rods that transform the light that reaches them into electrical impulses. These carry a set of data through the optic nerve to the brain. And from these data, the brain forms images. We really see not with the eyes but with the brain. A camera? It seemed to me that this process sounded far more complex than any camera, dazzling in its intricacy, with its mass of cells, circuits, and conduits suggesting a hopeless jumble but somehow following a sophisticated plan.

Sight is divided into two separate functions: peripheral and focal vision, the latter required for straight-on and detailed seeing. Focal vision originates in a small area, a quarter of an inch wide, at the center of the retina, called the macula. A sign of danger is the appearance in the retina of age spots, called drusen. Much of the time, these remain harmless, but they may also cause a thinning of the macula, until it atrophies, or "degenerates." This is known as the dry form of macular degeneration. The wet form, less frequent but more serious, occurs when blood vessels surrounding the macula break or leak and cause scar tissue to form. This may lead to the growth of new, abnormal blood vessels that are particularly fragile. When they break or leak, blood or other fluid invades the macula, causing further scarring.

My doctors told me I was suffering from the wet form. I tried to absorb all this with a journalist's curiosity, which, for the time being, was stronger than my apprehension. We have become accustomed to medical marvels: organ transplants, heart bypass operations, hip replacements. Concerning the eye, I knew about cornea transplants, cataract removals, treatments for glaucoma and other disorders that in the past had often led to blindness. I did not yet know how serious the effect of this disease could be, and I naturally assumed that it was treatable. But I was shocked to learn that it really wasn't—at least not with lasting effect. No comparable marvels had been devised for macular degeneration. I was outraged. Now I really started to worry.

The vision in my left eye was 20/400, well below the mark for legal blindness, which is 20/200. My right eye, on the other hand, was nearly normal at 20/30. What were the chances, I asked my doctors, of the right eye going as well? About 10 to 15 percent over three to five years, I was told. Those odds didn't seem too bad. My next question had scarcely occurred to me until then: What were the chances of my ending up totally blind? Very slight was the answer. But given the fact that six months before it had never entered my mind that I might have any vision problems, I did not feel reassured.

I was given a card showing a grid with a dot

in the center. If, when you look at the grid, its lines seem to waver or the dot seems to disappear, macular degeneration is progressing. Every day before shaving, I would stare at the card, first through my bad eye, then through my good one, nervously watching those lines and that dot. Normally, I welcomed the time I spent shaving as especially useful for thinking—about the day ahead, about calls to make and things to write. During my years as a journalist, I might start writing or editing a story in my mind while scraping away at my beard. Now I found myself thinking almost entirely about my eyes, trying to determine if I was seeing any less of my foam-covered face in the mirror. I could not detect any change. During the day, I carried the card with me in my wallet and would occasionally peer at it. For several months, the lines did not move, but then, just as I was becoming confident that my right eye was safe, the lines bent as if seen through heat waves. I rushed to my doctors, who spotted some bleeding in my right eye. They decided to try laser treatment.

This procedure consists of shooting a beam at the leaking cells in order to coagulate or seal them off, at least temporarily. It can be done in only about 15 percent of cases. The rest of the time, the damaged cells are directly under the center of the macula or very close to it, so that the beam could completely destroy focal vision. The laser had always seemed to me rather mysterious and menacing, an impression influenced by those early science fiction zap guns and death rays. I was nervous as I settled into my chair in the darkened room and faced the kind of machine I knew from my eye examinations. Now a laser device was mounted on it. My head was supported by a chin rest and held in place by a strap. On the other side of the machine was Dr. Guyer. His left hand, with the elbow supported by a fat sponge-rubber pad, held a tubular lens against my right eye. A special ridge on the lens allows it to be pressed safely against the eye surface, slowing down circulation and thus making it easier to seal off the targeted cells. (The device was developed by Yannuzzi and bears his name.) Guyer's right hand was on a joystick that would aim the laser beam through the lens at my eye. If that hand slipped, or if my eye moved, the laser could do serious damage. I felt helpless, totally under someone else's control. Guyer was entirely calm, working from the fluorescein picture taken earlier, which served as a kind of map. His voice was soothing as he admonished me not to move. Flash. My eye was struck by blinding light even stronger than the light I had experienced with the fluorescein pictures. His voice kept murmuring, "Good . . . fine . . . very good." This reminded me of the enthusiastic exclamations of professional photographers on a difficult shoot. Was he trying to reassure me that *I* was being good? Or did Guyer mean that *he* was being good? No time to ponder as more flashes exploded. After about three minutes, it was over. I remained dazed for nearly an hour. Later, I asked Guyer whether he had been nervous, too. "Not really," he replied. "This is what we do." Yannuzzi added, "Preparation . . . preparation, preparation is everything. Then it's like splitting a diamond."

2

I started to learn as much as possible about macular degeneration. But curiosity led me to a wider topic—the history of eye diseases and their treatment. I tried to follow medicine's long, difficult, and often quirky journey of discovery into the mysterious recesses of the eye. In early times, medicine and magic were more or less the same thing, and treatment might consist of incantations against evil spirits and magical potions. In the ruins of Nineveh, the capital of ancient Assyria, archaeologists unearthed thousands of clay tablet pieces dating from the time of King Ashurbanipal (668–627 B.C.), many of them dealing with the treatment of eye diseases such as trachoma (a potentially blinding infection), night blindness, corneal ulcers and scars, and tear-sac infections.

The water god Ea was also the god of healing;

water was used to cleanse a patient of demons, accompanied by appeals to Ea. One prayer went like this: "O clear eye, O doubly clear eye, O eye of clear sight: O darkened eye, O doubly darkened eye, O eye of darkened sight! O eye of sleepy sight . . . O painful eyes . . . like hay thrown away, like a cup of sour wine thrown away . . ."

There were also more mundane prescriptions. For dry eyes, "rub an onion, drink it in beer . . . disembowel a yellow frog, mix its gall in curd, apply to the eyes." For blood in the eyes, "reduce roses . . . in cow's milk or in the milk of a harlot . . ." Similar methods were used in ancient Egypt, where medication was apt to consist of copper derivatives, urine, saliva, honey, the whites of eggs, and the milk of a woman who had borne only boys. In Egypt as well as in Babylon and Sumer, surgery was also practiced, usually consisting of an incision with a bronze lancet. Surgeons and other physicians were subject to strict rules, patterned after the famous code of King Hammurabi. Punishment for malpractice was severe. A surgeon who bungled an operation on a slave lost his fee, but if it happened with a freeman, the law called for his hands to be cut off to prevent future mistakes. Similar conditions prevailed in India, where a type of cataract surgery involved quickly puncturing the pupil with a thin reed in order to move the cataract-damaged lens to the back of the eye. This highly risky procedure actually worked sometimes. Surgeons who botched it kept their hands but had their nose cut off. Doctors Guyer and Yannuzzi clearly faced no such jeopardy.

There was scant progress for centuries, although in the flourishing Muslim countries, Greek texts were preserved and translated. Greek physicians thought that eye diseases could be cured by drinking certain wines and by exercise, notably running. Hippocrates had many prescriptions for treatment, mostly mistaken. In some cultures, including the Greek, dreams were believed to heal; patients would dream that they had regained their sight, usually through the intervention of a deity, and would wake up the next morning, their sight restored. (I sometimes dream that I can see fully—people, scenes, pictures—but have never awakened to such a reality.)

In the Middle Ages, European scholars came to understand, and sometimes misunderstand, more about the lens, the retina, and the vitreous fluid that fills the eye, but they made no notable advances in treatment. In England in the thirteenth century, Roger Bacon developed the first known spectacles, although Romans suffering from near- or farsightedness had used curved glass lenses—Nero used a precious stone instead. One of the best-known eye surgeons, Guy de Chauliac (1298–1368), operated on cataracts by using an iron needle to move the damaged lens aside. As he did so, he repeated, "Our Father in Heaven, Our Father in Heaven, Our Father in Heaven . . ."

Toward the end of the eighteenth century, during Napoléon's Egyptian campaign, almost half of the French troops contracted serious eye diseases. These included swelling, inflammation, and discharges like those caused by gonorrhea, often leading to blindness. "The anguish of the afflicted is acute nearly to delirium," reported one chronicler. "The patient suffers the most excruciating pains, which are described as if the balls of the eyes were on fire, and the points of needles perpetually pierced into them." This medical disaster greatly contributed to the failure of Napoléon's campaign and gave a strong push for major eye research throughout Europe. But hardly any new forms of treatment emerged. Doctors still resorted to leeching, purgatives, and counterirritants, including poison. Many surgeons were reluctant to operate on the eye because the chances of success were slim. But the rest of the nineteenth century brought major advances, especially among doctors in Vienna, including better techniques for cataract extraction and the discovery that diabetes could cause vision loss. Drugs began to be used to dilate the pupil, enabling doctors to examine the inside of the eye effectively. Surgery began to be used for glaucoma (in which vision loss is caused by abnormally high pressure in the eye fluid). In New York, a surgeon replaced a damaged cornea with a cornea taken from a pig's eye; it worked only for a while. The young patient on whom the operation was performed, Alfred Lemonowicz, was recruited for vaudeville appearances—with the pig. Eventually, transplants from animals were abandoned. With the advance of modern medical technology, the cornea became (or so it seemed to me as I continued to explore the subject) a kind of experimental battleground. The small "seeing tissue" was subjected to every kind of incision, was sliced and planed and patched with donor tissue or synthetics.

World War II brought major progress. A British surgeon, Harold Ridley, at Moorfields Hospital in London, treated fighter pilots who had been injured when the plastic canopies of their planes were shattered by bullets during dogfights with the Germans. Shards of the plastic often penetrated their eyes, but Ridley noticed, to his amazement, that this did not cause serious damage. In fact, he found that these shards often actually improved a patient's vision because they refracted light. In time, this led him to develop a type of cataract surgery in which the scarred human eye lens was replaced with a plastic lens. (Eventually, I myself had this kind of operation.)

Scientists also began to learn more about the function of the eye not merely as a camera but as a portal of light for the entire body. The deprivation of light influences metabolic and hormonal processes such as sugar balance, water balance, blood count, and sexual function. Studies of explorers who spent long periods in the polar night showed, among other things, a decline in the metabolic rate, potency, and libido, as well as hair loss, insomnia, depression, and irritability. These symptoms began to disappear after the sufferers returned to normal light. It did not take science to illustrate the connection between light and mood. Richard Wagner once remarked, "If only the sun would come out, I would have the score finished in no time." George Bernard Shaw did much of his writing in a cottage that could be turned toward the sun—following the example of those primitive light-seeking organisms.

As for macular degeneration, it obviously always existed but was not separately identified.

Doctors simply assumed that it was part of aging, without doing much investigating of its causes or nature. Then in 1885, a Swiss ophthalmologist, Dr. Otto Haab (1850–1931), described and named the condition senile macular degeneration. There was little interest in the subject at the time, and Haab's reputation among his contemporaries rested on his development of a giant magnet to extricate foreign objects from the eye.

Despite Haab's identification, the label actually was applied to many other eye problems. Not until the 1970s did researchers achieve a clearer understanding of the disease. The pioneer in this effort was Dr. Donald Gass, for many years a professor of ophthalmology at Miami and Vanderbilt Universities. Lawrence Yannuzzi, his disciple, says, "Before Don Gass, there was no subdivision of retinal diseases. Of course, we didn't have fluorescein angiography. Gass was among the first to use that imaging technique. Until 1971 or '72, we knew there was bleeding but not why. We didn't understand the proliferation of blood vessels. At about that time, Gass started to describe conditions faster than we could try to cure them."

It has now been established that there are many different forms of degenerative macular diseases. Among them is the inflammatory variety, occurring especially in the Midwest and

Southeast, where young people sometimes inhale certain agents (for example, a fungus), which may lodge in the lungs for decades before spreading to the eye. There are hereditary forms—affecting mostly young adults with inadequate cells—including angioid streaks, little cracks in the back of the eye. These cracks are caused by an abnormality in the elastic tissue of the body which can affect other organs, as well. Then there is pathological myopia (sometimes known as extensive, or high, myopia), which also affects younger people. In it, the growth of the eye gets out of control; the back, where the macula is located, and the front develop differently, resulting in a bulge almost like an aneurism. Finally, researchers face the unexplained category known as idiopathic—"*Ideo,* meaning 'not enough information,' as in *idiot,*" explains Yannuzzi.

The symptoms in all these forms are different, but most of them involve scarring and bleeding, thus resembling age-related macular degeneration. Until recently, following Haab, it was identified as "senile" macular degeneration, but the word *senile* unjustly implied intellectual decline and so was replaced by the term *age-related.* It remains by far the most widespread type, but its causes are still mysterious. No one is quite sure why those cells break and leak, although there are many theories, none of them proven: genetics, smoking, high-fat diet, excessive exposure to sunlight, especially in people with light eyes and skin. The search for an explanation continues in countless places, a search anxiously followed by all of us who have the disease. I occasionally imagine that in some clinic or laboratory a scientist invokes whatever god of healing is currently in charge, reciting the ancient incantation: "O clear eye, O doubly clear eye, O eye of clear sight . . ."

3

After two months, my laser surgery was pronounced a complete success, with my right eye performing as well as when I first went to Yannuzzi and Guyer. Although the doctors warned me that improvement might not be permanent, I was beginning to relax, hoping that they had fixed my problem. But five months later, in September 1993, my sight began to deteriorate again, leading to another laser treatment. This time, I was much less nervous about the procedure itself but considerably worried about the future and how much longer I could depend on my eyes. I shifted between optimism and worst-case scenarios. I tried to picture what it would be like if my condition grew so bad that I could no longer read at all, watch a movie or television or a play.

My first reaction was bravado: "I could live with that, as long as I could still get about on my own," I announced. But I was less convinced than I must have sounded. I told my family only gradually about my condition, partly because I myself was learning about it only gradually and partly because I have always been reluctant to talk about any problems of mine. My children are sensible adults, but ever since they lost their mother, my first wife, Beverly, to cancer almost two decades ago, they have been concerned about my health. So I kept bulletins about any illness to a minimum. But Louise, deeply worried, insisted on meeting my doctors and interrogated them in her usual thorough fashion. She told my children, "Your father will probably never end up with a white stick, but still, this could become very serious." The mention of the white stick was a shock and alerted them to the potential gravity of my situation.

Soon afterward, my son, Peter, came to visit me. He was indignant. "As long as I can remember, you were always reading. That was the great pastime in our household. Maybe it was even an obsession." Referring to himself and his two sisters, he continued: "All of us read constantly— books, magazines, the instructions on medicine bottles. I simply can't accept that you soon might not be able to read and that there is nothing to be done about it. Am I getting this right? No one even seems to know just how bad things could get?" I had to admit that he had gotten it right. But we both took refuge in the thought that at least macular degeneration was not life-threatening. (Peter still has difficulty remembering the name of the disease, which he considers a subconscious form of denial.)

My daughter Mandy, who lives in Washington, was reassured by the fact that I kept going there on my own. But when she realized that my eyesight was deteriorating, she began to worry. "Every time I take out my contact lenses, it's a drag. The room looks dim and distorted. Is that the way it is for you? I can't imagine wandering around an airport like that." Actually, it wasn't all that difficult, because I knew where the shuttle entrance was at the airports, and the gate signs were large and illuminated. Still, I felt a small sense of accomplishment.

My daughter Lisa remembers having lunch with me at a coffee shop and taking the first uneasy steps toward adjusting to a father who was no longer quite the same. She felt oddly shy, not knowing how much attention I wanted her to pay to my situation. Would I want her to read the menu to me, or could I handle it myself? (I could with a magnifying glass.) How much did I want to talk about it? (Not much.) After we left, she was frightened as I crossed the street alone. When she told me about this, I realized that it was a moment that happens in most people's lives—the moment when the roles are reversed and the child must start taking care of the parent, rather than the other way around.

Gradually, I began to talk more readily and openly about what was happening to me. "There are worse things," I kept saying, and I would enumerate them—cancer, Alzheimer's, total blindness. A friend of mine once told me that at sixteen she wrote an essay about what it would be like if she had only one day left before going blind. She would not try to see things she had not seen before, but, on the contrary, would review the familiar: the foam on ocean waves, a squirrel in the park, the moon over the Empire State Building. I found myself repeating her fantasy. So much of what I was normally able to see was already fading. I became a visual glutton, devouring the images around me in order somehow to hold on to them before they grew even dimmer. The faces of people I loved—my wife, my children, my grandchildren, many friends. The chance glimpses of youngsters at play in Central Park, old men in peaceful combat playing chess in Washington Square. The Manhattan skyline in cold, pure autumn light. The Degas bronzes at the Metropolitan Museum of Art. Videos of favorite films (Katharine Hepburn in *The Philadelphia Story*, Laurence Olivier in *Henry V.*) The crystal chandeliers rising silently toward the ceiling at the Metropolitan Opera and, moments later, James Levine giving the downbeat. Old photo albums illustrating my life. The red sunset over Vineyard Sound seen from my summer house. A Thanksgiving turkey ceremoniously displayed on a platter, a plate of pasta sprinkled with flakes of white truffles.

I was far from alone. I found myself observing details of behavior in people that would not have caught my attention while my eyesight was normal. I noticed when someone was particularly careful walking down steps or when someone else was holding a menu very close to his eyes or looking at me in a somewhat vague, unfocused manner. Before long, I realized that these were signs of macular degeneration. Many people tried to hide it. An occasional pretense was to say, "How stupid, I forgot my glasses." Or possibly: "I just had an eye exam, and with these drops, I can't see a thing." Most were reluctant to talk about the real problem. But others, when they found out that I was also a "macular degenerate," were eager to compare our experiences. I began to feel that I was joining, involuntarily, a secret society.

For some months after my laser treatment, my condition alternately improved and deteriorated, depending, I was told, on the unpredictable and uncontrollable behavior of the cells in my eye. I was diligently swallowing vitamins, which my doctor said might not help but couldn't hurt, either. (Vitamins may reduce sun damage to the eye by lowering oxidation, but the link is not scientifically established.)

During a trip to India in January 1994, things got much worse. More than most countries, India is a marvel to the eye, but the dazzling colors and shapes grew blurred. The pushing, striving, overwhelming crowds in the streets seemed to merge into an indistinct mass. The brightly colored saris seemed to fade. The unreal aspects of the country became more unreal still. The graceful Palace of the Winds in Jaipur seemed to be all facade, like a stage set floating in the air. The Lake Palace Hotel in Udaipur struck me as a white mirage hovering over the water. The funeral pyres along the banks of the Ganges at Benares sent up clouds of smoke that appeared to me just as evanescent as the rest of the dawn-lit landscape. Even more disturbing were small incidents on the airplane that took our group from city to city. Fellow travelers would pass me newspapers or magazines or books about India with the injunction "This is very interesting; you've got to read this." I was already having difficulty reading, but I was still too embarrassed to admit it. I half-wondered whether a Hindu holy man might have a cure or some professional descendant of those noseless surgeons might wield a miraculous lancet.

Back in New York, I underwent laser treatment twice more. But an odd switch occurred. The right eye went down much further, while the left recovered to a degree. "Sometimes when one eye gets hurt, the other eye will kick in," explained Guyer. "When you have perfect vision in one eye, you don't use the other so much. When the right eye came down, the left eye used everything it had. It had it always, but didn't need to use it before."

I was advised to try magnification. Always a hopeless enthusiast for gadgets, I plunged into the realm of visual aids: magnifiers, magnifiers with built-in lights, reading lamps with lenses attached. I turned them and twisted them, held them close to the page and farther away. There were good days and bad days. A paragraph read was a triumph; a sentence undeciphered was a blow.

Reading and writing have been lifelines, as a source of pleasure and as part of my profession. I

went to *Time* magazine as a copyboy and immediately started writing stories, hoping to break
into print. Freely using the *Time* library and
office supplies, I joined with other copyboys to
launch a magazine of world affairs, a publication
that lasted for all of three issues. I also tried to
write plays, none of which ever came even close
to the footlights. At *Time*, I did make it into
print, for many years as a writer and later as an
editor. Over nearly two decades, I was managing
editor of *Time* and then editor in chief of all
Time Inc. publications. When macular degeneration set in, I had retired from Time Inc., finished
a stint as U.S. ambassador to my native Austria,
and was in the midst of writing my autobiography. My link with words was physical; I usually
read with a pencil in my hand. I often scribbled
notes in articles and books, even corrected mistakes of grammar or usage. Louise once observed
me on an airplane editing a story in *Newsweek*. I
once caught myself at a funeral correcting a mis-
print in one of the hymns. Now the words kept
receding and I tried grimly to hold on to them.

In search of "low vision" gadgets I went to
the Lighthouse, a gleaming renovated building
on Fifty-ninth Street between Park and Lexing-
ton. I had always thought of the Lighthouse as an
institution for the blind, where people made bas-

kets and other simple objects and where patients tapped along corridors with their white canes. I had not thought of it as a place for the merely half-blind or, in the awful jargon, for those just "visually impaired." I was surprised to learn that more than half of its patients are victims of macular degeneration.

When we are well, we rarely can see ourselves in an ambulance, in a hospital—or in a morgue. So, too, I had never imagined myself inside the Lighthouse. There, the signs are in large print or braille, the elevators audibly announce the floors, and, yes, one occasionally sees people with canes. A bright boutique there is full of magnifiers of all sorts, Scrabble and Monopoly with large letters, talking alarm clocks and watches with various voices. I auditioned them all and chose a wristwatch with the time announced by a pleasant, accent-free woman. There was even a talking scale, which gave my weight about forty pounds below what I knew it to be. With some regret, I decided not to buy it. None of this seemed morbid, but it told me that I was entering a different, confined world.

The Lighthouse is staffed with many skilled health professionals, including Bruce Rosenthal, a specialist in low vision. A bouncy, dynamic man, he presided over a huge inventory of visual aids. Full of enthusiasm for his wares, Rosenthal would always greet me with an eager "I've got something new to show you." Under his guidance, I experimented with monoculars for outdoor vision (the image usually quivers too much), binoculars mounted on spectacles for the theater or the opera, and extrathick glasses, requiring an object to be held no more than an inch away.

Querulously, I kept asking him why there wasn't more progress in this field, and I made eccentric suggestions, including the use of nightvision binoculars. They would be useless for macular degeneration, he replied, but he kept assuring me that all kinds of experiments were going on. One of these was LVES (Low Vision Enhancement System), developed at Johns Hopkins University School of Medicine in collaboration with NASA. It was a kind of helmet with tiny built-in TV cameras that enlarged the scene around the wearer. With its power pack strapped on, it proved heavy and cumbersome, giving me the sensation of being in a diving outfit on dry land. Much lighter and more sophisticated versions are in the offing. Less well known than the Lighthouse but enormously helpful is NAVH (National Association for Visually Handicapped). In its New York headquarters I found an even more dazzling array of magnifiers, lamps, and other gadgets, as well as a large-print library. But I had to accept the fact that, short of some extraordinary breakthrough, nothing can replace the infinitely intricate web of cells in the eye once those cells are destroyed.

4

Rummaging through a drawer one day, I suddenly found an eye staring at me. It was a small glass eye, which nestled in a miscellany of old key chains, identification tags, and tiepins, the sort of useless objects I have a hard time throwing out. The glass eye was a charm I had picked up years before during a trip to Greece, where—as elsewhere in southern Europe and the Near East—such amulets are widely used as protection against the "evil eye." I dangled the glass orb in front of me and its black pupil seemed to fix me with vague menace. Long forgotten, the thing now fascinated me. It was a reminder not only of the evil eye myth that runs through many civilizations, but, more generally, of the role the eye has played in mythology. I started to supplement my sketchy knowledge of this by turning to books, either plowing through the pages myself, with increasing difficulty, or having passages read to me. This excursion was a welcome escape from the enervating business of experimenting with magnifiers and obsessively checking my eyesight. It brought me some comfort, as well as entertainment.

Since earliest times, man imagined the eye in the heavens. It hovered over ancient civilizations like the sun. It was considered the all-seeing, all-knowing instrument of the gods. Having gotten through approximately one-third of Norman Mailer's *Ancient Evenings,* I was prepared for rampant mystification of the eye in old Egypt. I was not disappointed.

Horus, the god of the sky, had one of his eyes poked out in a struggle with a rival god, but it was later restored to him. The healed eye symbolized the victory of life over death, the reconciliation of darkness and light, and it was painted on the inside of coffins to enable the dead to see in the next world.

Less concerned with the afterlife, but very much concerned with the authority of their single God, the ancient Israelites considered the eye as a symbol of the all-powerful, all-seeing but unseeable Yahveh. The prophet Zechariah saw Yahveh symbolized by a stone decorated with seven eyes, representing His watchful presence. Ezekiel saw the wheels of Yahveh's chariot decorated with open eyes, signifying divine omniscience.

In Hinduism, one god was known as the eye of the sky, another as the god of a thousand eyes who sees everything. In one version, the sun was born of the eye of a cosmic giant. But in Hinduism and Buddhism, as well as in other religions, the eye was not merely an agent of divine surveillance. It was also considered the center of human wisdom and insight, known in various forms as the inner eye, the third eye, or the eye of the heart. In Greek religion, too, the eyes of the gods were everywhere. Kronos had two eyes in front and two in the back, while the rest of the pantheon had different but equally powerful vision. The single eyes of the giant cyclopses were useful not only for their work as armorers to the gods but also for striking terror in lesser beings. Their gaze was worshiped as well as feared. Athena's eyes were piercing and relentless. When Achilles angers her, she forces him to look into her face and he cries, "It is terrifying to see the light of your eyes."

Paradoxically, the gift of wisdom and prophecy connected with the inner eye often went with loss of outer vision. Blindness was sometimes regarded as a punishment for someone having seen the forbidden. Tiresias, the blind seer of Thebes, was deprived of his sight because he had observed Athena bathe. Another version has it that the gods had temporarily turned Tiresias into a woman and then back into a man. In their perpetual soap opera, philandering Zeus and ever-jealous Hera asked him to settle a dispute about which sex derived the most pleasure from love. When Tiresias answered that it was the female, Hera was scandalized and blinded him. On the other hand, Zeus gave him wisdom. In the Oedipus legend, Tiresias reluctantly tells the king that he has unwittingly killed his father and married his mother. Refusing to believe this enormity, Oedipus berates Tiresias as a "crafty beggar" and tells him that he is "blind in your ears, in your mind, and in your eyes." When it turns out that Tiresias has been telling the truth, the king puts out his own eyes, saying, "Why did I have to see when there was nothing I could see with pleasure?" In one interpretation of the familiar story, I found a twist that was new to me: The king should not have insulted Tiresias, because the Greeks believed it was wrong to mock the blind as well as the dead, since the blind were regarded as quasi-dead. It was a chilling thought.

(It occurred to me that in modern myths, novels, and films, the old contrasting ideas about sight and sightlessness live on. Blind characters are often feeble or villainous, symbolically linked to death. Or else they are heroes, gifted with sensitivity and special powers, enabling them to "see" much more clearly than the sighted.)

Having trudged through a good deal of Teutonic legend during my Austrian school days, I half-remembered many tales about the eye. One concerned Odin (aka Wotan), who cast one of his eyes into the well of Mirmir in return for a sip of its immense wisdom. His son Balder supposedly represented the handsome and kind side of his father, while the other son, Hodr, represented the blind spot and the deadly side. Another myth involved the Basilisk, a legendary monster with a lethal glance. It was said to look so horrible that if a mirror was held in front of its face, the creature would be so frightened by its own image that it would explode. When I first heard that story in my boyhood, I considered it quite comic, but I realized later that it was a version of the evil eye. The belief in it remains widespread, based on the notion that the eye—especially a misshapen or squinting eye—can transmit hate, revenge, and bad fortune. Against this force, preventive magic must be used in the form of charms, signs, and incantations. The evil eye is, perhaps, the ultimate tribute to the power of sight, although

Christianity has always condemned it as rank superstition.

Christian teaching opposes the evil eye with what might be called the "Holy Eye." It connects the eye with the divine light, the "eye of the heart" with the ability to see God. The Desert Fathers, contemplative hermits who lived in the Egyptian desert in the fourth century A.D., proclaimed, "Man must become entirely eye." Perhaps the most touching Christian homage to the eye centers on St. Lucy (the root of the name means "light"), a virgin and secret Christian who lived in the time of the Roman emperor Diocletian, when Christians were hunted down by the authorities. She was betrothed by her mother to a pagan but refused the match, insisting on giving herself to God. According to legend, she was betrayed by her scorned suitor and tortured. Presumably, her eyes were put out, because statues show her holding a dish with two eyes in it, but according to another tradition, her sight was miraculously restored. Lucy became the patron saint of the blind and those with poor vision.

I did not believe that my macular degeneration was punishment for having seen forbidden things or that it brought me any special wisdom. But amid this whole welter of myth and legend, it was pleasant to encounter Lucy. Even if she could not do much for me, and although I am Jewish, I was pleased to have a patron saint of my own.

Science has long ago demythologized the eye, but not entirely. I found the account of its evolution so fantastic that it might as well be mythology. Even Charles Darwin felt that way.

"The eye to this day gives me a cold shudder," he wrote in 1860. He meant that its development was what any layman would consider miraculous and was difficult to explain through evolutionary theory. The evolution of any living organ from primitive beginnings—often no more than an impulse, a piece of hardened skin, a muscle—to the most complicated mechanisms defies the imagination. That is especially true about the development of the eye. It suggests an endlessly patient and ingenious experimenter trying out various models, discarding some and improving others, gradually producing devices of ever-growing complexity.

The first organs that could be called eyes probably developed from those light-sensitive cells on the skin of primitive organisms, known as eyespots or stigmata. Some of these cells presumably grew in a recess or pit of the skin and a tiny hole over this recess allowed light to enter. This is the principle of the "pinhole eye" still found in creatures like flatworms and mollusks. These cells gathered in clusters, together forming a simple eye, or ocellus. Such eyes are still found in insects and leeches. In the nautilus, a primitive eye is bathed by the ocean to wash away obstructions (in human beings, this cleansing function is re-created by tears).

In time, a protective membrane grew over the eye pit, eventually acting as a light-focusing lens. Each type of lens functions differently in gathering, enlarging or reducing, and bending light signals, and sending them on to masses of photoreceptors and through nerve threads to a brain. The variety that developed is dizzying. The butterfly lens, for example, is basically the same, on a tiny scale, as a two-lens astronomical telescope. A scallop has over one hundred eyes, each containing a lens.

A different model—a different experiment— was the compound eye, which may have first appeared a billion years ago, on tiny three-lobed creatures at the bottom of the sea. It consisted of a cluster of individual stems with light receptors at their tips and able to spread out for a wider field of vision. Such compound eyes still exist in many animals, including the housefly, which carries several thousand seeing stems. The fiddler crab, while buried in the sand, can raise its eyes on two stems like periscopes. From such beginnings, eons led to the sophisticated eyes of vertebrates with their specialized functions—powerful long-distance vision, enabling hawks and eagles to descend on the smallest prey; night vision in nocturnal creatures like the owl and the cat. Three-dimensional eyes with depth perception were necessary for primates to walk upright, enabling them to use their hands for wholly new activities, which in turn led to an enlarged brain. Thus advanced sight was indispensable to the emergence of human beings as we know them.

What made Darwin shudder was the notion that all this could have happened through natural selection. The theory is familiar: Accidental changes in an organism produce an advantage—a clearer lens, more powerful muscles, greater dexterity—that enables the organism to survive. These traits presumably are passed on to future generations by inheritance and thus gradually shape new life-forms. To suppose that this process, beginning with a dab of pigment, could have produced "the eye with all its inimitable contrivances for adjusting the focus to different distances, for admitting different amounts of light, and for the correction of spherical and chromatic aberration," wrote Darwin, "seems . . . absurd in the highest possible degree." Nevertheless, he insisted that this is exactly what happened. The seeming absurdity produced not only shudders but disbelief and rage on all sides. Still no convincing scientific explanation has replaced Darwin's version.

Through specialization, runs this theory, the eye adapted to different conditions. Hunter-gatherers needed long-range vision to spot their prey and their enemies, and the most farsighted survived. When men took to agriculture, long-distance vision remained important, but less so. With the development of handicraft and reading, sight was concentrated on ever-nearer objects and myopia became an indicator of modern life.

A kind of evolution also takes place within each human being. We are born with the potential of seeing, but we only gradually develop that potential. A newborn's eyes are uncoordinated and see only as far as eight or ten inches. Slowly, the baby develops binocular vision—using both eyes together—permitting him to judge distances. In time, he learns to recognize objects and faces. Hearing and touching remain the dominant senses for a while, but by age two, the eyes take over through a process of trial and error. By age four, the child can maintain eye contact and recognize what he sees between ten and twenty feet away. In the words of the late Dr. Arnold

Gesell, a leading authority on child development, "A child is born with a pair of eyes but not with a visual world. He must build that world himself and it is his private creation."

I started to recall how I went about that process of creation and I found it a compelling exercise in memory, an autobiography of my eyes.

5

The very first sight I could recall was the yellow-and-white-striped wallpaper in my nursery and the border just below the ceiling with its running depiction of *Puss 'n Boots.* The recollection suggested something about the connection between sight and memory, and the mysterious nature of memory itself. Why did this particular image etch itself into my brain and not others—some rattle or teddy bear, my mother's face, or the plants that probably were at the window? The brain and its instrument the eye play an ever-puzzling game without discernible rules. Or could it be that there really *are* rules and we simply don't understand them?

I tried with almost manic concentration to recapture other details of those earliest years. One clear recollection was a drawing a friend of my older sister Meta made for me showing the family car and our driver, whose name was George ("Gog" as pronounced by me). I realized that the rather simple pencil lines did not *really* look like the car or George. But I accepted them as true, my first lesson that one sees not only with one's eyes but with one's imagination. When I tried myself to draw, I learned another, related lesson; while I thought I knew just what I wanted to render, the crayon or the pencil in my hand simply would not follow the outline in my mind. I understood later that this is not merely a childish experience but that it expresses the infinite gap between seeing and creating. I retrieved other visual memories. The intense pleasure of looking at stacks of shiny colored paper—many colors, each producing a different sensation. (Years later, I had an art teacher who tried to convey the musical overtones of various hues. "Blue," he would coo seductively, or "red," he would shout aggressively, rolling the *r* with gusto.)

Looking at letters was a special experience. Long before I knew how to pronounce them, or to write them, I saw images in them: the cozy roof of a capital *A;* the wide face of the *O,* which, when a little line was added at the bottom, turned into an animal with a tail; the serpentine *S,* which I disliked even before I saw and dreaded my first snake. And when it came to fear, nothing frightened me more when I was very small than St. Stephen's Cathedral in Vienna, whose huge black spire struck me as some overpowering monster. But far more often than fear, learning to see brought delight. Among those delights were my first visits to the theater, where I fell forever in love with the contrast between the brightly lit scenes on the stage and the dark auditorium, and was almost hypnotized by the beam of a spotlight reaching through that darkness. I remembered the joy of being shown a kaleidoscope and my wonder at seeing those infinitely various shapes forming and re-forming themselves in mysteriously symmetrical patterns.

It occurred to me, as I was trying to recapture and hold all these visual memories, that I was constructing in my mind a kaleidoscope of the past: the intensively satisfying gleam of brass fixtures. The solid, purposeful, but sometimes mysterious shapes of tools in a handyman's kit or in a hardware store (I have been addicted to hardware stores all my life). The beauty I perceived in machines—locomotives, automobiles—which in the years of my growing up seemed more elegant and in a sense more human than the far sleeker versions later on.

I became intrigued with optical instruments and by the act of looking through a small aperture, which seemed to promise entry into a secret domain. I was stunned by my first look through a microscope and the bustling life that took place in a few drops of water. But before that, I doted on binoculars, which, in the rural slang of Austria, were known as *Zuwizahrer*, or, roughly, "drag-it-close." I sent away for an object I had seen advertised; called the Little Spy, it was a very small telescope. (Remembering it, I realized ruefully that it resembled one of those monoculars that Dr. Rosenthal at the Lighthouse had shown to me.) It was not especially powerful, but I pointed it constantly at the scenes around me. The river near our summer house, shimmering in the morning sun. At the clouds overhead, in which, like all children, I imagined seeing all kinds of shapes—camels and castles. I peered at mountaintops and they, too, suggested images— a prone woman or a crouching animal. These were childish games, but they did suggest something about how sight and fantasy go together. If nothing else, such tricks of the imagination helped me to remember later what I had seen.

I realized that my little telescope was useless in surveying the night sky, and I would tilt my head back to look at the stars until I grew dizzy from that posture and from the futile attempt to understand infinity. I certainly did not need my spyglass to explore the intricate splendors of the roses in our garden, the glowing patterns of the butterflies I caught—and of girls. I became aware of their soft round cheeks, their curls, their sometimes graceful, sometimes tomboyish movements—their essential differentness. It would take years before I looked at them more expertly and more purposefully.

Traveling with my parents, I became fascinated by the constantly changing glimpses of the scenes rushing past the train window, and I tried to hold the fleeting images in my mind. I saw my first glacier, white shading into blue, a vast and nearly blinding expanse. I saw Venice in dazzling, bright, hot summer light, its ornate gray structures strange and confusing, its greenish canals too implausible for me to recognize their beauty. On later trips, I learned to appreciate the overall harmony achieved by the seemingly clashing and bizarre buildings, the mysterious labyrinth of little streets, where turning any corner might bring a surprise, the promise of adventure on a fog-shrouded evening.

I was taken to museums and churches and heard grown-ups talk about "a Tintoretto" or "a Michelangelo" without comprehending the reverential tone with which they pronounced those names or the works that were pointed out to me.

I was first drawn to the most realistic pictures and thought that "It looks just like a photograph" was praise for a painting. I gradually learned better. When I was ten or so, my parents gave me, as a birthday present, a simple box camera. Taking pictures became a lifelong addiction. Looking through a viewfinder was even more exciting than peering into a microscope or through a telescope. Photography is a special form of seeing the world, but it can also be constricting. I have sometimes tried so hard to frame a picture in just the right way, to catch a view from the right angle or in just the proper light, that I have lost sight of the overall scene. I could never see an arch, an oval window, an opening in a hedge, without posing somebody within those frames, thus achieving a quite artificial effect. But the camera also sometimes produces unintended results. I remember taking pictures of a lake in Austria and, once the film was developed, being surprised to see in the foreground the play of waves, patterns of light and shadow, which I had not observed when I took the pictures. Photography can form an accidental conspiracy with the eye that delivers more than one expected. For the skilled photographer, of course, this is not accidental at all. Composition, lighting, and focus create far more than copies of nature. "Like a photograph," I learned, is not a synonym for "realistic."

Somewhere in my reading, I came across the story of the artist who was painting a tree and was approached by a farmer who asked, "Why do you paint this tree, since it is there already?" The answer was, or should have been, that the serious artist—or photographer—does not copy reality, which is mere appearance, but something beyond appearance, something that is in his soul or in another realm. Still, I was captivated initially by sharp-edged representation and by dramatic contrasts. I loved those qualities in Georges de La Tour, but if one looks at his canvases for a while, it becomes obvious that the interplay of light and darkness, of bright colors and shadows, creates not drama so much as an enigmatic stillness. I came to experience some works as one experiences certain people or places that one longs to see again and again. Fra Angelico's glowing saints; El Greco's tortured, elongated cardinals; Dürer's preternatural, almost spiritual precision; Rembrandt's combination of vividness and solemnity that he brought to his burghers.

I found in Turner unique lessons in subtlety and mystery, precision behind a veil. Looking at his haunting seascapes, I had the feeling of seeing them through half-closed lids, through a mist. Ironically enough, this anticipated the way I came to see after I developed macular degeneration; Turner's canvases of Venice resemble the way I now see Venice—and everything else—as if through a haze. I began to wonder whether Turner himself might have had an eye problem. As far as we know, he did not and his style was quite deliberate. But I eventually discovered that many artists were plagued with failing vision, and not only in old age. They include Michelangelo and Piero della Francesca. I became particularly intrigued by the experiences of two artists, Degas and Monet.

Degas was bedeviled by eye problems for most of his life. The trouble began when he was only thirty-six and found "a spot of weakness" in his eyes. Serving in the National Guard in 1870, he could not see a rifle target through his right eye, and he later blamed the cold and damp he was exposed to as a sentinel during the siege of Paris by the Germans. Visiting relatives in New Orleans two years later, he complained of the intense bright light of Louisiana and painted almost entirely indoors. After the visit, he was alarmed and gloomy. "I shall remain in the ranks of the infirm until I pass into the ranks of the blind," he wrote to a friend, and to another: "I envy your eyes which will enable you to see everything until the last day. Mine will not give me this joy." He experienced a blind spot in the center of his vision and found it excruciatingly difficult to draw around that blind spot. Painting became an "exercise of circumvention," recalled an artist friend. No records exist to show precisely what caused Degas's deteriorating vision, but his self-diagnosis involving cold and damp was probably wrong. One friend remarked that the artist was suffering from "chorioretinitis," which in the nineteenth century covered a variety of diseases, including macular degeneration, not yet identified at the time. But chances are that he was suffering from some form of retinal degeneration, possibly hereditary. As he continued to work, his sense of color faded and he sometimes asked his models to identify the colors of his pastels. In his later work, his colors grew increasingly garish compared to his earlier subtlety, and forms grew less precise. His friends and admirers were deeply sympathetic to his suffering, but some suggested, maliciously, that he was exaggerating his condition to avoid greeting people he did not want to speak to or so as not to have to attend exhibitions by other artists. Perhaps I am prejudiced by my admiration for him, but I doubt that he used such fakery. Perhaps I am also influenced by my own experience, because I would gladly talk to people I don't like or view pictures that bore me if only I could see them clearly.

When Monet found that he was losing his ability to distinguish colors clearly, his first reaction was, as he later described it, defiance. "How many times I stayed for hours under the harshest sun sitting on my campstool . . . forcing myself to resume my interrupted task . . . wasted effort. What I painted was more and more dark . . . and when the attempt was over and I compared it to my former works, I would be seized by a frantic rage and slash all my canvases with my penknife." It turned out that Monet was suffering from cataracts, and one ophthalmologist after another proposed surgery. But Monet was afraid of that. Finally, at the age of eighty-three, he agreed to a cataract operation on his right eye. A terrible patient, he had to be restrained from tearing off his bandages in a rage, and later he kept fighting the special glasses he had to wear. Since he refused to have surgery on his left eye as well, he saw differently through each eye—he could perceive violets and blues with the right eye but not with the left. He was again able to read and write clearly, a condition that I and other sufferers of macular degeneration can only envy, but Monet was not satisfied with that because it did not amount to the kind of vision he needed as a painter. He felt that he should really give up painting altogether, but he could not. He kept on working, although it was torture to him and he produced much that he considered mediocre, much that he destroyed. But eventually, his vision improved dramatically, thanks to adjustments of his glasses (the doctor prescribed a black lens that covered his left eye entirely). He once again painted with joy and said that he would like to live to be one hundred. He died at eighty-six. Only two years earlier, he had written, "If I am condemned to see nature as I see it now I'd rather be blind and keep my memories of the beauties I've always seen."

I would not rather be blind, but I do cling to my memories of what the adventure of seeing was like before the twilight of macular degeneration set in. There were certain habits and rules I had developed about looking at art—which often apply also to looking at life. I thought of them as the art of seeing. We don't usually think of it as an art, taking it casually. Diamond cutters, ship captains, bird-watchers, stargazers, proofreaders, and artists use their eyes with discipline and precision. Most of us, most of the time, use our eyes superficially, without seeing nearly everything there is to see. Looking is not seeing. As my disease progressed and the reality around me grew increasingly hazy, I kept recalling what the experience of normal sight had been like and what I had learned, sometimes unconsciously, about how to see.

6

The first rule in the art of seeing was that one must see not only with the eyes but with the imagination, a lesson I learned as a child when I looked at that primitive drawing of the family car. To that lesson, I soon added the principle that one must not be constrained by labels. From what I had read about Watteau, for example, I expected to find elegance, amorous dalliance, rococo superficiality. Yet there is more beneath the surface.

Looking at *Gilles*, the picture of an actor in white silk, without preconceived notions, one finds a different and disturbing note; the actor looks fixedly front, as if waiting to speak, but also as if waiting for a sign. To some, he appears dazed and naïve. Yet his eyes also convey patience, experience, a touch of cynicism—the eyes of a man who has seen everything, surrounded by men and women who see only one another. This actor sometimes seems the only real man in Watteau's world; the "real" people look make-believe.

There is always the question of the role played by reputation. Prejudgment and bias can determine what one sees, not only in a museum but in life. Is it better to know that one is looking at a great master's picture, or is it better to experience the picture without foreknowledge? Is it better to be thoroughly instructed before viewing a painting—to know, for instance, that the dove symbolizes the Holy Ghost and the lily the Virgin Mary—or simply to be exposed to the work? I used to find it more satisfying to be without special background at first viewing, merely to absorb the faces, figures, scenes. Even the untutored eye, if it is linked to a minimum of reflection, can sense the religious quality of the stylized, almost impersonal faces of Early Christian painting and the gradual emergence of the secular, human portrait, which marked the advent of individualism. Equally unmistakable is the move of the Annunciation and other religious scenes from celestial or rustic settings into bourgeois interiors. But sooner or later, information is indispensable. One's eye can appreciate only part of *The Judgment of Paris* without one's knowing that it is Paris who is handing the apple to Venus, and ultimately receiving Helen of Troy as a reward, thereby starting the Trojan War. Seeing Castagno's *Last Supper* is enhanced by the knowledge that the ominously dark piece of marble embossed with a flash of lightning is just behind the head of Judas. I liked to read up on art after seeing it, rather than listening to even the best taped lectures while walking about a museum, because they forced me into seeing things only in a certain way and a certain order.

Often choices must be made—for instance, between trying to look at everything or allowing oneself to be dazzled by one work of art until it becomes a part of one's soul. When Mandy Patinkin was preparing to play Georges Seurat in Stephen Sondheim's *Sunday in the Park with George,* he spent weeks sitting in front of the painting *Sunday Afternoon on the Island of La Grande Jatte,* until he felt that he knew enough about the people in it to have painted the picture himself.

La Grande Jatte makes a special statement about the relationship between details and the whole. It is filled with many figures and objects, together creating a harmonious scene. One must pay as much attention to the parasols as to the monkey, the cane, the fishing pole. The simple lesson is that there are no unimportant details in a good picture.

Ironically, when Patinkin was studying *La Grande Jatte,* he was looking at it through diseased eyes. He was suffering from keratoconus, in which the cornea thins and then bulges out, interfering with vision. For years, Patinkin was able to see normally, thanks to corrective contact lenses, but eventually he was told he would have to have a cornea transplant to save his vision. He received the cornea of a thirteen-year-old child and then became a touching advocate for organ donations. "I wonder who he was and what he saw," says Patinkin. "I will pray for him the rest of my life. I often think I am not looking through my own eyes; I'm looking through a child's eyes."

One of the characters in Proust's *Remembrance of Things Past,* the writer Bergotte, comes across a review of Vermeer's *View of Delft,* which he thought he knew well. But he could not recall a particular patch of yellow wall, which the critic claimed was rendered so well that it could stand by itself. The writer, though fatally ill, drags himself to the gallery to gaze at that yellow patch, which mesmerizes him.

In many pictures, the artist spreads out the details or the figures evenly, leading one to read, as it were, from side to side or top to bottom: the crowded scenes of Brueghel's village life, Bosch's bizarre scenes of hell.

Most of the time, however, the artist tries to force your attention by highlighting a face or object and subordinating other elements to the main focus. If the artist wants to capture the eye with a gleaming spot on the helmet as in *Man in the Golden Helmet* (long and perhaps mistakenly attributed to Rembrandt), so be it. But one should sometimes rebel against such persuasion and let one's gaze wander to background, dark corners, details, minor figures, because they, too, are there for a reason.

These principles also apply to the art of seeing the daily world. I have usually tried—and it is not easy—to meet a statesman, tycoon, or movie star without constant awareness of her or his status and the trappings of power and glamour, and to try to read somehow the underlying characteristics of a face or a personality.

And when watching a play, I was apt to repeat what I did in seeing a painting; my eye would wander away from the central action to the shadows, the dark corners, the lesser figures, the walk-ons, even the bookshelves on the wall or the silver tea service on a table. This is more difficult to do in watching motion pictures because the camera in effect becomes your eyes. It thrusts you into a close-up of lovers kissing or a truck rushing toward you. But even in film, it is possible for the eye to stray to surrounding detail and incident. Does this represent a distraction? Yes, but it is a necessary distraction to experience the fullness and ambience of the scene. A similar truth holds in daily life. The bric-a-brac in a living room may tell as much about people as their appearance or their speech.

Nature provides more such lessons. A beach is not only a sweep of sand but shells of sea creatures, the sea glass, the seaweed, the incongruous objects washed up by the ocean. It is also an insistent reminder of change and of the need to look many times, for a beach is never the same from hour to hour or day to day. It is possible to miss the forest for the trees, but the greater danger is to miss the trees for the forest, to miss the individual sunflower for a whole field of sunflowers. That phenomenon is reinforced by the speed of modern travel. When railroads became widespread in the nineteenth century, many people complained that the landscape was rushing past so quickly that the pleasure of attention to individual sights was lost. "It matters not whether you have eyes or are asleep or blind, intelligent or dull," said John Ruskin. "All that you can know, at best, of the country you pass is its geological structure and general clothing." And again: "A turn on a country road with a cottage beside it, which we have not seen before, is as much as we need for refreshment; if we hurry past it and take in two cottages at a time, it is already too much. . . ." Undoubtedly, Ruskin would have felt the same way about the automobile, and the jet plane would have driven him to despair.

The eye sends a billion messages each second to the brain, twice as many as the whole rest of the body. Yet sight is often reinforced by the other senses. A rose looks different when you can smell it. A ballroom looks different when you hear music. Whenever I saw the Arc de Triomphe in Paris, I would be apt to play the "Marseillaise" in my mind, and the monument somehow seemed grander and more real.

The scent or the melody helps the image to stay in the mind long after the object itself is no longer there. A sidelong glance can evoke powerful images: A glimpse into a lighted window at dusk has sometimes given me a full sense of domestic serenity; a half-observed glance or gesture between two people at a party can instantly convey the hint of a secret love affair. But usually seeing requires time, especially when one looks at that most telling and infinitely varied scene—the human face.

Manners are apt to prevent us from looking at a face too directly or too long. So does lack of interest. We walk through city streets intent on our own concerns, paying only the most casual attention to the faces and figures we pass. Yet we know that faces tell stories and we casually decide that someone looks angry or troubled or amused. But we don't often focus on the signs that signal these emotions or their degree and shading. Frowns, laughs, yawns are obvious, but we are apt to miss the more subtle indicators—the quick compression of lips, the brief furrowing of the brow, the fluttering eyelid, the averted gaze. Watching so intently may suggest the lover or the interrogator, and this can make people uncomfortable. But I have always found it better to err on the side of too much attention rather than not enough. It takes time to get to know a face, but once it happens, there is a special satisfaction in the mutual readings of one another's moods and thoughts.

Women's faces are an endless delight—and mystery. I find it extremely difficult to describe them, perhaps more difficult than describing anything else. One can follow the shape of a mouth, the width and angle of a nose, the color and position of eyes, but such details do not add up to a whole. The total effect, the spirit, remains elusive. Countless words have been devoted to capturing the Mona Lisa, but her appeal remains enigmatic. The world is full of living Mona Lisas. Again, it is not just a matter of what the eye sees but also what the mind brings to the act of seeing. The judgment of beauty—or ugliness—is shaped by long-vanished experiences, dim memories, dreams. Perception is an individual process. As any reporter, detective, or artist knows, two people can look at the same face or the same scene and see something quite different. Perception may be altered with fashion and with one's own changing tastes. In my teens, I was utterly captivated by the fresh round doll face of Alice Faye, who flourished in 1940s films, and the pert, gamine look of Ginger Rogers. It took some growing up before I could appreciate the colder symmetries of Garbo's features or the slightly masculine planes of Dietrich's mask. In my adolescence I found guilty pleasure in the fleshy women of Rubens and not until much later did I appreciate the thin, somewhat angular women of Klimt. Ultimately no representation, no picture, can substitute for the direct and immediate experience of life. A woman's face is never more amazing than in the climax of sexual passion, when it may combine joy and pain, satisfaction and protest in ways that make it seem for an instant like the face of a stranger.

Macular degeneration has deprived me of much of this visual experience: the really close observation of faces, scenes, pictures. My explorations in the art of seeing now exist mostly in my recollections. These days, I cannot walk into a museum without vowing during the first fifteen minutes that I will never visit a museum again— the experience is simply too frustrating. Pictures are dim puzzles. Viewing a battle scene, I might recognize a waving banner or a rearing horse but cannot make out the melee of fighting soldiers or the shapes of the fallen. Looking at some allegory, I have a hard time determining whether a nude figure is male or female. Faced with the *View of Delft*, I cannot find that yellow area that so transfixed Proust's character. Rembrandt is mostly undifferentiated gloom except for the occasionally sharp highlight, and in Fra Angelico I can discern the robes of a Madonna but not her features, can spot the child but not read its face. And yet after awhile, my frustration fades, at least in part, as does my initial determination never to return. Many pictures still have meaning for me. If a painting is well lit and if I can get very close to it, I still see a great deal. Many portraits, like the ones by Titian or Memling, seem to burst out of a fog and seize me with sudden power. The same is true of Georges de La Tour's sharp contrasts and Vermeer's illumined details. I perceive many of Cézanne's well-outlined figures, even if his still lifes elude me. Memory and imagination help but also confuse. Looking at *La Grande Jatte,* I am not sure whether I see or only remember the little monkey, or, looking at an El Greco, whether I see or only imagine the elongated, anguished contours. As for Turner, I see his haze through my own haze but find that even this doubly dim impression is better than none at all. I have also discovered the virtue of those guiding tapes that I once disdained; with Philippe de Montebello's words in your ear at New York's Metropolitan Museum, even vaguely seen works come to life. And so, never without some dread, I keep going back.

7

Living with macular degeneration means living in a half-veiled world. I can still see a sunrise, mountains, buildings, can, in fact, see almost everything—but as if through a scrim. I often have difficulty identifying people. Arriving one evening at a Chinese restaurant in New York with family and friends, I walked up to what I took to be the maître d' and tried to shake hands. My son, Peter, tapped me on the shoulder and said, "Who's your friend, Dad?" The large statue of a monkey did not return my greeting.

Once in Paris, accompanying Louise to a couture house, I strayed into the fitting room by mistake. Before I beat a hasty retreat, I noticed a half-dressed woman trying on a gown. A few minutes later, Louise emerged from the fitting room and said excitedly, "Did you realize that was Catherine Deneuve?" I had not. I have adored the actress for years at a distance, and here I missed the chance to see her close-up—very close-up.

I find that often I don't even recognize old friends and seem to cut them dead; at other times, I greet total strangers as old friends. At a party several years ago, I walked up to a tall, striking blonde and was on the point of saying, "Hi, Diane." I thought I was facing my friend Diane Sawyer but stopped myself at the last moment when I heard someone addressing her as "Ma'am" and realized that I was confronting Diana, Princess of Wales. When I come upon Louise in conversation with someone, she finds a pretext to repeat the name.

Just to be on the safe side, I now return any greeting with enthusiasm, which usually pleases and sometimes puzzles acquaintances. In fact, people who have heard about my problem introduce themselves to me, even when I recognize them perfectly well thanks to strong lighting, or from their voice or their shape. One of the difficulties about macular degeneration is that those around you can never be sure what you see, and you yourself are not sure, either.

Faces are apt to be a blur or they entirely disappear. I am sometimes reminded of a movie, *The Invisible Man,* with its shots of the hero's face and figure gradually vanishing.

Most of the time, it is impossible for me to tell whether someone is smiling or frowning and whether a woman is pretty or not. The intense pleasure of watching women has become much diminished for me and is possible only with close and well-lighted proximity. Once at a cocktail party, I found myself talking to a woman in a dim corner whose engaging voice and lively movements suggested to me that she was young and beautiful. When I told my hostess about this, she laughed and said, "Henry, that vision of yours is too creative. The lady is pushing seventy and far from beautiful."

I have had similar experiences since, and I eventually told myself, "What's wrong with seeing beauty that isn't there?"

Reading faces and the signals of mood and temper, which I had taken for granted as part of the art of seeing, has become extremely difficult except when I'm inches away. Eye contact is nearly impossible, which eliminates a vital form of communication. "As a mother," my daughter Lisa told me, "I am less upset that you can no longer scan the damn newspaper—I know you can get the news in other ways—than that you have a hard time seeing my childrens' faces." When my granddaughter Elizabeth went through a shy period and relied on smiles and nods to respond, Lisa firmly explained to her that I needed to hear her voice because I could not see her expression. Sometimes I seem abstracted to people—"out of the moment," as my children put it—but, in fact, I have learned to compensate by listening more attentively than ever (I have always been a good listener) and I can quickly make out fatigue, sadness, or anger from someone's voice. I have trained myself to look in the direction of voices. This is difficult when several people are talking at the same time, but I find that I can handle conversation at the dinner table and the conference table well enough.

It is hard to distinguish colors, and I pick my shirts and neckties under bright lamps, usually asking Louise to ratify my choices. She is often amazed, as am I, that I have come up with a pleasing combination. But I sometimes get it wrong. As we were leaving for the opera not long ago, she suddenly realized that I was wearing brown shoes with my tuxedo. When I appear wearing one black and one blue beach shoe, as has been known to happen, I simply announce that I am trying to start a new fashion.

When I drop a coin or anything very small, I usually have a hard time retrieving it. But occasionally—and I consider this downright perverse—I can spot a tiny object on the floor. A

doctor explained to me that I was probably looking slightly sideways on those occasions, moving
the blind spot in my macula out of the way.

Once when my son, Peter, came to see me, he
was surprised that I did not notice that he had
started to grow a beard. On the other hand, I was
able to spot that one of his shoelaces had come
undone. "I'm never sure what you can and cannot see," he complained. "That makes two of us,"
I replied.

Shopping or window-shopping is difficult. I
often find it impossible to tell a camera from a
tape recorder from a radio. A shop window full of
shoes can look like a candy store and a cleaner
can look like a deli. I have walked into a ladies'
room thinking it was the men's room because I
could not decipher the letters or the often quaint
symbols for male and female on the door. When I
see someone combing her hair before a mirror,
I mutter an apology and flee. Stairs are a hazard
and the care necessary to keep from stumbling
creates an air of decrepitude I loathe. When steps
are familiar or in a bright space, I skip down
them ostentatiously. I must concentrate constantly to avoid tripping over curbs, rugs, or
other low obstacles, which is extremely tiring.

The eye enables us to reach out into life. It
means freedom, independence. The lack of that

independence is disheartening. Many people's reaction to macular degeneration is denial. They continue to handle money without being able to see it clearly, stab at the wrong elevator buttons, and even drive cars far beyond the point of safety. I also went through such a period. I would wake up in the morning, turn off the alarm clock, and open my eyes. Everything would be in place: the windows and doors, mirrors, desk, dressing table. It all looked a little hazy, but that seemed natural in the subdued morning light. I would get out of bed, put on my glasses, and pick up the day's paper, looking at it, hard. The words were a blur. For moments, I simply refused to believe that I could not read.

Nor would I believe that I could no longer easily find the tip of my cigar with a match or readily locate ashtrays, paper clips, or scissors on my desk, which became more chaotic than ever. Eating became a particular problem. In the illumination found in most dining rooms or restaurants, food in front of me was nearly indistinguishable. I have been known to bite into a lemon assuming it a shrimp, or to try to slice a bone as if it were meat. The loveliest presentations are lost on me, but this has not diminished my sense of taste or my appetite. Unfortunately, food is difficult to coordinate with knife and fork and so I seem to have entered a second childhood of messy eating. Finding a salt shaker on a table is a major challenge, and wineglasses are in danger of being upset by my uncertain hand. I have sometimes reminded onlookers of a deep-sea diver laboriously reaching for scarcely visible objects. The need to ask for help was at first excruciating. I would grope on a platter to serve myself at table, unsteadily picking up three potatoes and no meat. The opposite could also happen. At one dinner party, when I helped myself from a serving dish being offered, the maid whispered to me, "Mr. Grunwald, you have taken the meat meant for your entire table."

I might stand for five minutes in front of an airport monitor, trying to decipher the gate number of my plane before finally asking someone. Eventually, I had to change my attitude, however reluctantly. At a street corner, I would no longer hesitate to ask a passerby whether this was Sixty-eighth Street, and on a plane if the seat numbers were too small, I would no longer shrink from asking another passenger whether this was 16B. Of course it was humiliating, but I came to terms with the fact that in some situations it is foolish not to ask for help. At the same time, I recognize the temptation to take the easy or lazy way and let somebody else do things for me that with some effort I can do for myself.

I move around New York as much as ever, but with a healthy caution crossing streets. I slavishly wait for the light to change (I can usually see that) even if there is no traffic, and I have taken to crossing alongside other pedestrians—especially women with baby carriages, next to whom I feel very safe.

I travel widely, and during a trip to Egypt, I crawled into tombs with a flashlight resembling a miner's lamp strapped to my forehead—which only partly enabled me to see the hieroglyphics. I scrambled around the fabulous ruins of Angkor Wat but often needed to rely on the strong arm of a guide. Taking photographs remains my hobby. Although I use a camera with an extralarge viewfinder, I sometimes decapitate people. I am especially careful not to do this to our dog, Harry, whose picture I usually take each year for our Christmas card. In the theater, I miss many of the details, but telescopic lenses attached to my glasses enable me to follow most of the action. In the movies, I sit as close to the screen as possible—which means that I can find a seat when the rest of the auditorium is full. Some of what happens in the film eludes me and I am apt to confuse the hero's face with the villain's or to be unsure whether a certain shape is a corpse or a sofa. Subtitles are almost impossible to read. But I do follow the plot. (As with movie subtitles, I cannot read the English text scrolling past my seat at New York's Metropolitan Opera, but even with works I don't know well, the music and the singing make up for it.) When I watch television, my head is almost up against the screen.

Our society is increasingly trying to help people with impaired vision. Experiments are going on with a system called Descriptive Video Service (DVS), which can provide audio descriptions of television and movie scenes through special equipment. The U.S. Treasury has issued new fifty-dollar and twenty-dollar banknotes with larger, more legible numbers (many critics find them aesthetically unappealing, but they are useful). At least one hotel in Manhattan has a special suite for sight-impaired guests, equipped with large telephone keypads, magnifying mirrors, decor with contrasting colors, and furniture with rounded edges.

My greatest frustrations involve reading and writing. After a lifetime during which these activities were as natural and necessary as breathing, I now feel the visual equivalent of struggling for breath. The world of words in which I had always functioned has become drastically altered. We receive 80 percent of our information through the eyes (or so the experts tell us), and a significant part of that still comes from the printed word. Not until my vision problems developed did I realize just how dependent I was on reading in various forms, not only for work and pleasure but in countless other ways: scanning magazine cover lines as I pass a newsstand, trying to find a name and floor on a building directory, deciphering labels in the medicine cabinet, glancing quickly through correspondence. Such fast sight bites are now usually beyond me.

At first, I had the weird sense that this was somehow slowing down my mind. I don't think it did, but the mental effort needed to absorb anything like the same amount of information I did when my eyes were intact is considerable—more so than I realized at first. I read labels, addresses, menus, with handheld magnifiers, which takes time. I bought a magnifying machine, which is essentially a closed-circuit TV set. A camera focuses on the text and blows it up on a screen. Thus I can read as I move the text back and forth under the camera, but this is laborious and slow. Much of the time, I lack the patience to read that way.

I turned increasingly from the written to the

spoken word. Having long used recorded books during trips or stretches on the treadmill, I now gradually came to do all my book reading that way. Apart from commercial services in that line, there are excellent nonprofit sources, including the Library of Congress, the Heiskell Library in New York, and the Reading for the Blind program. Most publishers offer taped editions, often abridged, of many titles. Poor readers can be a trial. But, paradoxically, the better the readers are, the more they tend to create their own impersonations of the characters, which can be quite different from the characters in one's own imagination.

I keep up with newspapers and magazines in various ways. Some services offer readings from newspapers and books through special radio receivers, but one cannot select the subject or the timing. The Internet carries the texts of many newspapers and other reading matter which can be listened to with audio software, but this requires help with using a computer. Therefore, I have hired readers to record newspaper and magazine articles on tape. (I am fortunate to be able to afford this.) Where I would once open the paper in the morning to scan the headlines, a reader now does this for me and I choose the stories I want to hear. I listen to the tapes on a Walkman whenever and wherever I can—walking, riding in a taxi, before going to sleep. This works well enough, but it is almost impossible to skim on a Walkman as one does with print, and this is extremely frustrating and inefficient.

At first in conversation, I found it difficult to say, "I read this article," because it would give people the wrong idea of what I was capable of doing. On the other hand, "I have heard this article" seemed silly. I compromised by using such phrases as "I have come across this piece."

I acquired an impressive machine, really a combination of a scanner and a computer, into which I can feed pages and have them read back in a synthetic voice. (As a matter of fact, there is a choice of several voices, male or female, soothing or high-pitched.) Despite occasional glitches, it is a help, but I still rely on human voices, especially my wife's.

Being read to at length is still strange; I have not had the experience since childhood. It often makes me feel helpless and passive. Occasionally, my mind wanders. One regular reader tests me for attention by slipping some outrageous statement into the text to see if I will react. I sometimes want to linger over certain passages and skip others, but it takes a very special reader to be so adaptable. Fortunately, Louise is. As she reads to me tirelessly, week in and week out, she is quite willing to skip. But she rarely bypasses a day's papers, and if we fall behind, she insists on catching up. "You never know what you will miss," she says. "And anything I like, I want you to hear."

I know living with someone in my condition must be a trial for Louise. She denies it or cites only minor irritations. We've had to give up our marathon Scrabble games (I have a hard time making out even the enlarged letters available at the Lighthouse), and I had to stop reading bedtime stories to her. Dr. Dolittle used to be a favorite. When we do double acrostics, to which we are addicted, Louise has to do all the pencil work. The letters and spaces are tiny and I often lend her one of my magnifiers. She rarely complains about the difficulty, but she once told a friend, "I hold myself back from saying things like 'Oh my God, after an hour of this I feel like I'm going blind.' "

I am sure that Louise understates the problem, and I was confirmed in this belief when I met a remarkable man who has a sensitive appreciation of how a relationship can be affected by a handicap. He is Nick Stevenson, the founder and head of a support group, the Association for Macular Diseases. An affable, energetic former sugar broker and World War II veteran, Stevenson was a company commander in the First Marine Division in the landing on Guadalcanal. He has suffered from macular degeneration for seventeen years. Despite his handicap, he travels tirelessly across the country organizing symposiums about how to deal with the affliction—especially its emotional consequences. "Here is a disability totally unprepared for, totally unexpected," he says. "Now one of the horses is not pulling its weight and we feel badly about that. And the other horse resents the additional duties—without saying that."

Stevenson continues: "We have an obligation to others. We like to think that the world has an obligation toward us because we have the problem. We would like the world to slow down and say, 'I understand you have a vision problem. We can rearrange our schedules. You're a valuable player; we can do things for you.' But the world doesn't. It moves on faster and faster."

8

I heard Nick make these remarks at one of the many free seminars he conducts all over the country. This one took place in Pearl River, New York, a hamlet about an hour from Manhattan. Most of its approximately fifteen thousand inhabitants work in civil service, and at the pharmaceutical plants in the area, or own small businesses. (The village was founded in 1872 by one Julius Bronsdorf, who, according to local authorities, invented the incandescent lightbulb but was beaten to the patent office by Edison.) The setting for the meeting was the Senior Center at the Masonic Temple. An overflow audience of more than one hundred people gathered about round tables covered with pertinent literature and sign-up sheets for the association. At one end of the hall, coffee and Danish pastries were available, while at the other end, there was a display of various reading machines. In the lobby, elderly people were playing bridge and poker, obviously not afflicted by vision problems. Inside the hall, the crowd was paying close attention to Stevenson.

"There is a strong tendency among us to go from doctor to doctor, hoping to find one who will say, 'Of course I understand; macular degeneration; here is what I'm going to do.'" But, Stevenson made clear, no doctor can say that, because the disease is still unexplained and mostly untreatable. "We feel ourselves infinitely less independent and more vulnerable than once we were. . . . When our roles with our families and friends change, we feel we are no longer dealing with them as absolute equals, but it is still important to keep those relationships close. . . . Often when our families offer some magnifying device, it's easy to say, 'No, I've tried this and it doesn't do any good.' We have to smile and say we'll try it and that it might be just what we need." (I fear I am not always as tactful about this as Nick would wish.) "Friends ask, 'Did you see in this morning's paper?'" Nick continued. "You learn from experience not to say, 'No, I don't read anymore.' Say this a few times and it makes our friends uncomfortable, guilty that they can still see, while we cannot."

What advice would we give to others in the

same boat? Stevenson asks rhetorically: "Surely it would not be to sit down on a chair and give up. Willing or not, we must fare forth: We must remain part of the world."

Stevenson's audience seemed quite prepared to take this advice, or at least to try to. The questions at the end, which he handled with great patience, were practical, realistic, and free of self-pity. The very fact that these people had made the effort to come to the meeting showed that they were not giving up, Stevenson said later. He quoted, with a smile, the famous remark that "eighty percent of life consists of showing up."

Not the least impressive fact about Nick Stevenson's talk was that he gave it fluently, forcefully, and without a note in front of him. This reminded me of my own struggles with making speeches.

In the past, I would usually speak from a written text. That is no longer possible, even with a TelePrompTer. I must do without a script or even cue cards in front of me. (Notes in letters large enough for me to read are too cumbersome.) I had always enjoyed making speeches, but now I felt a tension I had not experienced in years. Out of habit, I would stare down at the lectern as if the words might miraculously rise up in front of me, or I would survey the blur of the audience, wondering whether my nervousness made *them* nervous. At first, I tried to memorize a whole text, but I found this too difficult, partly because it made for a stiff and hesitant delivery, as I was trying to remember every word. Now, for short talks, I work out in my mind what I want to say and then simply speak off-the-cuff. For longer efforts, I dictate the whole thing, then read it over with magnification or have it read back to me several times. I might memorize certain key parts. When I give the speech, I move from point to point; if I skip one, I attempt to work it back in along the way, as in a conversation or in telling a story. This is far more difficult than it sounds, especially when facts and figures are involved, and I'm still working on it.

There is a vast difference between absorbing the written and the spoken word. In Plato's dialogue *Phaedrus,* the god Theuth complained that the discovery of writing "will create forgetfulness in the learners' souls because they will no longer use their memories. . . ." He was probably right, in the sense that most of us now need the written word to sustain memory. I have always retained what I've read more securely than what I've heard.

Another difference between reading and hearing is more subtle. I thought of the written or printed word as something solidly constructed or sharply etched, while the spoken word seemed evanescent, written on air. To the eye, *meretricious* and *jurisprudence* are difficult and rather ugly; to the ear, they can be melodious. Seen, "To be or not to be" appears choppy; heard, the words are mellifluous and poetic.

I became aware of this because macular degeneration set in while I was writing my autobiography. I worked on my word processor as long as I could, but when it became too difficult, I switched to dictation. I was accustomed to dictating letters, speeches, articles, but talking a book was another matter. Every line had to be read back to me or printed out in very large type. For the most part, I tried to visualize the text on a mental page. I often found, on hearing my words, that I had been prolix and repetitive, and I had to edit myself. A highly literate friend predicted there would be a discernible difference between the parts I had written and the parts I had dictated. I hope he turned out to be wrong. Other friends tried to reassure me by telling me that Henry James had been forced to dictate his later novels (the language was increasingly dense) and reminding me of many writers, from Milton to Aldous Huxley, who were blind or nearly blind. I was touched when I learned of Huxley's attempts to find compensations in his affliction. "Being able to read braille," he said, "I can read with the book beneath the blankets. So my hands are kept warm on even the coldest nights." (I have not tried to learn braille—not that anybody has suggested it to me. In my mind, it implies total blindness and would mean a denial of the sight I still have.)

For most of these writers, dictation was the obvious way to continue their work. That is why losing sight is less awful for a writer than it is for a painter. Jorge Luis Borges, who lost his sight progressively, beginning in childhood (blindness ran in the family), painstakingly dictated both poetry and prose. Having worked out a line or a sentence in advance, he would dictate five or six words and have them read back immediately. During the reading, his right index finger would move across the back of his left hand as if following on an invisible page. The same words would be read back again and again, until he was sure how to continue. After two or three hours, he might have produced half a page. Borges often wryly commented on his condition. Referring to his position as head of Argentina's National Library, he wrote in one of his poems about "God's splendid irony in granting me at one time 800,000 books and darkness." He once observed,

"When one cannot read, then one's mind works in a different way. In fact, it might be said that there is a certain benefit in being unable to read, because you think that time flows in a different way. When I had my eyesight, then if I had to spend say half an hour without doing anything, I would go mad. Because I had to be reading. But now, I can be alone for quite a long time. . . . I don't have to be talking to people or doing things. . . . I wouldn't feel especially unhappy or lonely."

Another writer who tried to find some compensation in loss of vision was James Thurber. When he was six, his brother accidentally shot him in the eye with an arrow, and despite innumerable operations, his condition gradually grew worse, until he was totally blind. At first, he was angry. He compared himself to a blindfolded man looking for a black sock on a black carpet. "Life is no good to me at all unless I can read, type and draw. I would sell out for 13 cents." He was irritated by what he considered the widespread ignorance about eyesight and was amazed that people actually offered to give him one of their eyes, as if such transplants were possible. Eventually, he accepted his situation and learned to dictate easily; he usually composed fifteen hundred words in his head before he started.

Unlike sighted writers, he said, he was never distracted by people or scenes around him when he was trying to work, not suffering from the "handicap" of vision.

With at least outward humor, he listed some of the benefits of failing vision.

He would see a cat rolling across the street in a striped barrel or bridges rising into the air like balloons or a "little old Admiral" riding a bicycle. All these were ordinary objects that his failing eyes turned into fantasy. "The kingdom of the partly blind is a little like Oz, a little like Wonderland," he wrote. "Anything you can think of, and a lot you never would think of, can happen there."

I sometimes have similar experiences. Riding in a car at night, I might see the moon, only to find it is really a streetlight, or a conflagration that is really a neon sign. But for me, the kingdom is not nearly as enchanting. Fantasies based on faulty vision do not delight me and I don't welcome the soft edges of reality; I miss the hard edges. I find it unsettling not to be able to make out the details of my own face in the mirror. Nor do I share the sense of timelessness and lack of pressure that Borges described. On the contrary, I tried to prove to myself that I could do as much as ever—writing, keeping up with magazines and newspapers and books, working for nonprofit organizations—and I reluctantly had to face the fact that I could not do it all.

Sometimes I rub my eyes and stare, feeling that I must be able to pierce the misty curtain around me—but of course I can't.

I am still on close terms with the written word, although it has become a very elusive companion. I can still write in longhand, slowly. My handwriting was always chaotic, but now, especially when I print, the result is actually clearer than before. I try harder. I am forever searching for new low-vision gadgets, most of them only partly helpful—a large magnifying glass suspended from a cord around my neck and propped against my midriff, freeing my hands; a jeweler's loop with its own light that fits like a visor around my head. I had often heard that as one loses vision, other senses take over. I found this only partly true. In handling objects—sharpening a pencil, plugging a lamp into an outlet—I rely far more on touch than I used to. I am drawn to music, but that is not new for me, since music has always been a love of mine. In fact, paradoxically, I am faced with a new difficulty: I used to listen to music while reading, and this is no longer possible, since I now do my reading mostly through listening. But for all that, the will to see remains as strong as ever, and I sometimes imagine that I keep struggling toward vision like those one-cell organisms straining toward the light with their eyespots.

Books haunt me. I still habitually pause in front of any bookstore window and I'm still shocked every time I find that I cannot read the titles. When my autobiography, *One Man's America,* was due to be published early in 1997, I would eagerly walk to my neighborhood bookstore, Madison Avenue Bookshop, hoping for a display of the book. When it did appear, someone had to tell me that it was there, because I could not make it out. Still, it was a very gratifying moment.

I occasionally walk into one of those huge book supermarkets like Barnes & Noble and Borders to inspect the piles of volumes, which somehow convey a reassuring, even exciting sense of plenty. Here I can pick up a book, hold it within range, and read the cover and title page. But that is about all. People around me browse, reading a paragraph here or a page there, but I can no longer do that.

The same is true at home, but even more intensely. Books are everywhere in our apartment. As I look at the book-filled walls, they seem to give off a stubborn silence. The books mock me or thrust me into nostalgia. I know that those four volumes on the second shelf from the top are a history of the Crusades that I used to dip into often. Over there, I recognize from memory Churchill's history of World War II. In the fiction section, a half a dozen Nabokovs and countless beloved P. G. Wodehouses. Yes, I could pick up any of these, place them under the enlarger, and read—slowly. Even a short passage is frustrating, and the notion of reading a whole book that way overwhelms me. I think it would take almost as long as it would take those legendary monkeys to write *Hamlet*. When I do pick up a book and leaf through it quite pointlessly, I come across my old scribbled notes in the margins or on the endpaper. True, I would have a hard time deciphering them even with perfect vision. As it is, they are hopelessly obscure, hidden as if in an unbreakable code, a recollection of the times when books spoke to me silently and I to them. But do I clean out those shelves? Do I eliminate the books? I cannot, and I absurdly add new ones. Books, they say, furnish a room. My books are still more than furniture, but less than the living things they used to be.

9

Macular degeneration did not condemn me to the equivalent of polar night, but it did make me restless and moody. Several fellow sufferers told me that they had sought help from therapists but found that few, if any, were expert at dealing with our problems. A notable exception, I heard, was Dr. Josephine DeFini, a psychiatric social worker and Clinical Director of Social Work and Independent Living Services at the Lighthouse. I eagerly got in touch with her.

She confirmed what I already knew about denial. "Vision loss is like falling from the throne. When people first suffer from macular degeneration or other impairments, the reaction is usually disbelief. . . . 'I *can* see,' they will insist. They put themselves in difficult situations, like taking the subway alone. Or they will displace problems on something else, like claiming that a sign is in the wrong place or someone has moved a piece of equipment. Sooner or later, when this does not work, terror sets in." People become depressed, although they don't always realize it. Some withdraw and merely vegetate. Most become deeply angry—at life, at people with full vision, at anyone trying to help. The therapist's task, said Dr. DeFini, is not to respond to the anger but to show that, within limits, help is possible.

The first time I spoke with Dr. DeFini was on the telephone. She vividly described her work with macular degeneration sufferers—telling me about the wife who refused to go to parties with her husband because she had trouble recognizing people, and another woman who stopped going to restaurants because she was embarrassed to be observed eating sloppily. (I understood this well.) In the midst of her discussion, Dr. DeFini suddenly said, "Oh, by the way, I don't know that you're aware of the fact that I myself am blind."

I was stunned. The possibility had never occurred to me because she had talked so casually of organizing meetings, traveling, supervising her staff of about thirty, who work with approximately four thousand clients. She even spoke of what she "saw" in her patients. Dr. DeFini mentioned that it does not help many people with impaired vision to tell them, "You won't go blind." I asked her whether she did not grow impatient with people like myself who complained about merely limited vision loss. "I haven't felt that way for a long time," she replied. "The reality is everyone's situation is unique. . . . When you are blind, you have no other picture of yourself to present and the community sees you as that. With partial sight, you can create confusion. And you live with the fear of waking up one day with no sight at all. Once you've lost it, there are no more questions."

Josephine DeFini lost her sight at eleven as a result of detached retinas that surgery failed to correct. Until then, her vision had been poor, but nobody had realized it and her slowness in school had led to the belief that she was retarded. She had hated school, and when she became blind, her first reaction was relief that she would never have to go back again. But she did, and with remarkable speed she learned braille in a public school and also used talking books. "I began to flourish. Since I was the oldest and the quickest, I read to other children. I developed an ego."

As she moved toward her successful career (Dr. DeFini has worked at New York's Beth Israel Hospital Metropolitan Center for Psychotherapy and is also in private practice), she discovered a

principle she would pass on to her patients: She
had to help the people who wanted to help her,
to teach the people who wanted to teach her.
Therapists who have never themselves experienced the loss of sight have difficulty treating the
sight-impaired. "You can say to the sighted doctor," she tells her patients, " 'I want to teach you
how to understand and deal with me and what I
need from you.' " This applies in many situations
other than therapy. When Dr. DeFini started taking Spanish lessons, she found that the instructor
used a great deal of body language. She explained
to the teacher how to translate those movements
into words.

During our telephone conversations, I had
recognized DeFini as strong and confident; that
impression was greatly reinforced when I met
her. She proved to be tall, statuesque and elegant,
with a warm and outgoing disposition. She is
usually accompanied by her guide dog, Clancy, a
twelve-year-old Labrador who is suffering from
poor eyesight herself, in addition to several other
ailments. But DeFini will not give up on the dog
("I am one to always push the limits"). And
Clancy has shown no signs of giving up, either.
DeFini moves with great assurance and is quite
unself-conscious about her condition. I watched
her having her picture taken and she asked, with-

out the least embarrassment, for someone to point her in the direction of the camera. Asking for assistance does not faze her.

As I well knew, some people have a hard time accepting help. This is often true of immigrant patients—especially Asians, in DeFini's view—who are apt to be too proud to want to admit a disability. It becomes a matter for the whole family, which is likely to try to hide the affliction. Americans on the whole are far more open and feel that they have a right to be helped.

Dr. DeFini tells her patients, "I can't put your vision back, but I can let you know that you're not alone and can help you find other options." When people say, "I can't read" or "I can't cook," they really mean, "I can't do it the way I used to," and she tries to teach them that it can still be done, if differently. "What the person needs is to relearn. People don't think enough about how much knowledge they already have, how much experience. They function in families, in the community, and in life."

Just how people can relearn is demonstrated by the many classes in independent living supervised by DeFini. I visited one such class at the Lighthouse. I half-expected to intrude on painful struggles, frustration, perhaps even despair. Within minutes, however, I was caught up in a normal, casual, and cheerful atmosphere. The class took place in a large windowless but brightly lighted room with two kitchen installations at either end, one with an electric and the other with a gas range and oven. In the center, around a long rectangular table, sat three men and four women. They were a retired dentist, a dental technician, a medical secretary, a hospital food supervisor, a retired typesetter, and two housewives. The scene reminded me of a home economics course of a kind popular in the fifties, except that the participants were long out of school, their ages ranging from forty-three to eighty. Three out of the seven had macular degeneration, while the rest suffered from other forms of eye damage. The task for the day was to prepare lunch—chicken with broccoli and potatoes. The chicken was already cooking amid appetizing smells. I wondered how the seasoning had been done and was told that spices were identified either by smell or by simple touchable markings on the containers. The group around the table was now peeling potatoes. Some used peelers with ordinary steel handles; others used implements with specially padded grips, making it easier to bear down on the potato. Those with enough contrast vision could see where the skin was coming off and the potato was clean. Others were peeling by feel; the clean part of the potato felt smooth and the rough part was the skin. When it came time to cut the potato in quarters, the clients were told to form a bridge with their thumb and forefinger and then to cut inside that bridge. This kept the blade away from the hand. I was moved by the immensely detailed care with which the three instructors supervised these efforts. There followed advice about boiling water safely (whistling teakettle preferred), about using the ovens with long-sleeved mitts, about turning the stove on and off by following tactile markers placed on the controls. A typical class meets three times a week for four weeks, after which an instructor usually visits the clients at home once or twice to help them adapt their skills to their particular way of life, including not only cooking but sewing or gardening or exercise. No detail is too small to deserve attention. Instructors explain how bills of different domina-tions can be folded in special ways so that they are easily picked out of a wallet, how socks of various colors can be marked with different configura-tions of small safety pins, how medicine contain-ers can be identified with two, three, or more rubber bands, how checks can be written with a plastic template whose cutouts guide the pen.

Again and again, I was struck by the lighthearted mood in the class. The common experience of impaired vision not only created a strong bond among those around the table but provided a sense of relief. Being together with others who had the same problems and understood what it was like to learn a new way to perform the most elementary tasks brought great comfort and camaraderie. After the classes are over, many members bond so strongly with one another that they are invited to come back to form a support group with the advice of a social worker. I remembered something Nick Stevenson had told me: "It is very lonely to be with people who do not share your affliction."

Overcoming that loneliness has been the aim of the Lighthouse from the beginning. It was started by two young sisters, daughters of the publisher Henry Holt. He urged the older one, Winifred, to go to work as a volunteer at the Settlement House on Delancey Street, which in the early years of the twentieth century was surrounded by poverty and misery. She quickly made it her mission to help the poor, and she begged money from family and friends. One of her projects was to construct a fountain to bring clean water to the neighborhood. With it, she later wrote, "came a flood of happiness to my perplexed heart. At last I felt I had a right to existence."

During a trip to Europe a few years afterward, Winifred's social conscience found a new object. Attending a concert in Florence, she observed a group of young blind boys listening raptly to the rather indifferent performance. "When we return to America," Winifred Holt told her sister, Edith, "we must see that the blind have music."

Back in New York, they tried to raise money for the project, but nobody took them seriously. Finally with a borrowed four hundred dollars and their dress allowances, they started the New York State Association for the Blind, Lighthouse Number 1, located in their home. (Winifred affectionately referred to this rather grandly named organization as "old ass.") Its principal service at first was to provide concert tickets for the blind, but the sisters soon found other ways to help. Dealing with the sightless at the time was starkly simple; in New York the blind had a choice between the poorhouse or a pension of fifty dollars a year. Begging was assumed to be a natural occupation for them. Putting the blind to work was considered not only impractical, what with all the new and complex machinery out there, but inhumane. "Some went as far as to say that it would be cruel to add to the burden of infirmity the burden of labor," Edith Holt wrote later. "As if to be without work were not the heaviest burden mortal could be called upon to endure." At a public meeting to raise money for the Lighthouse in 1907, Mark Twain, a family friend, said, "They ought not to be compelled to subsist on charity. We would give them an opportunity to earn their bread and know the sweetness of the bread got with the labor of one's own hands."

The Lighthouse itself was soon staffed by blind switchboard operators and typists. As the organization grew and was replicated in many foreign countries, the aim increasingly was to put the blind to work. That aim inspired the formation of the Lighthouse workshops, which received sizable government subsidies. The workers made not only brooms and mops but sheets, machine parts, plastic "relief bags" for the air force, and dozens of other items. At first, the workshops were regarded as progressive and liberating, but more recently they have been seen by many as restrictive. In 1994, the board of directors decided to abolish them (although some continued under different sponsorship). Barbara Silverstone, a gerontologist who was appointed to head the Lighthouse in 1984, explains: "The philosophy of the Lighthouse is that you work side by side with sighted people. There is no need for the blind or those with partial vision to be in a special environment. We have people going out of here every day getting competitive jobs," says Silverstone. "We teach them certain keyboard skills and how to use adaptive equipment."

For the most part, this equipment consists of computers with special software that talks. Instructions to and from the machine not only appear on the screen in the normal way but are also heard through a sound synthesizer. In certain models, the words the operator types are simultaneously read out. Some of this high-tech equipment was on display at a Lighthouse function I attended, which resembled a trade show plus social get-together. People with every degree of impaired vision stood in clusters chatting or strolled about inspecting the devices being demonstrated on tables along the walls. Some of the demonstrators were sighted; others were blind and were accompanied, like many of the visitors, by their gentle, patient guide dogs. Among the exhibits was a copying machine that took a flat drawing and rendered its lines in raised form that could be followed with one's fingers. There was a special computer attachment that produced printouts in braille. I saw a computer-scanner that read out any text in a synthetic voice, just like the one I had at home. The operator was blind and handled the device effortlessly, but at one point, when the computer froze, she calmly asked a sighted visitor, "Let me borrow your eyes for a moment. Tell me what message is showing on the screen."

Much of the mission of the Lighthouse is devoted to training its clients (they are not called patients because they are not under the care of medical doctors). Employment counselors, often with a marketing or head-hunting background, work aggressively to place people in all sorts of jobs. They have succeeded especially well with airlines, where Lighthouse graduates work as reservation clerks; with telephone companies; and with Off Track Betting, which has many people with diminished vision taking and checking bets.

These employment efforts are particularly important because, as Barbara Silverstone says, "young people do not want to work in workshops anymore. They don't want to be stereotyped, limited in their opportunities." But when the Lighthouse accommodated these ideas by eliminating the workshops, "we were criticized, because there was a culture of the blind we were supposedly deserting."

Among the critics was one of the stalwarts of the Lighthouse, Dr. Eleanor Eaton Faye, an ophthalmologist who has worked there for forty-three years. A floor of the building is named in her honor. Highly independent, she never formally went on staff, because she wanted to be free to say and do what she pleased. She has also been in private practice and taught at several institutions. (My doctors were among her students, Guyer in seminars at the Lighthouse and Yannuzzi at the Manhattan Eye, Ear and Throat Hospital.) Many of the blind, she points out, are afraid of competing in the outside world, where they are apt to be patronized, at best, or avoided by other workers and fellow students. They cling to what she calls the "blindness system," with its protective environment and special benefits. This often applies even to people whose vision is only partly gone. Dr. Faye tells of a young patient whose eyesight was impaired since birth. He went to ordinary public school but came to the Lighthouse for a recreation program. He told her, "I don't mind going to a school where kids tease me, but I'm so relieved to get here on Saturday and have my program with the blind kids. I can relax."

With the Lighthouse now sending so many people out into the world, Dr. Faye misses the old warm sense of community. "It used to be kind of a folksy place where everyone knew everyone, where all the workers and the blind people came. They had a home, where they felt cozy."

Most professionals in the field today would side with Barbara Silverstone rather than with Eleanor Faye. For better or for worse, Silverstone's attitude conforms to the spirit of the times. The difference in the two views reflects the difference in society at large, with the newer view insisting that no one should be segregated and all should be treated equally, including the handicapped. The difference also suggests a kind of relativist view as opposed to an absolute view of blindness (and, by extension, life in general). Pointing out that almost 90 percent of Lighthouse patients have some vision, however slight, Silverstone, like other experts, insists that there is really a continuum from blindness to merely low vision. Dr. Faye is uncomfortable with the notion of continuum. She considers it merely a way of talking about a very complex subject and believes that "blindness is a real marker." On this point, I agree with her.

I can still see and presumably could continue to see, at least minimally, even if my condition were to grow worse. But it seems obvious to me that somewhere along the line there could come a flat separation between seeing something and seeing nothing.

Whatever differences exist between those who want to "mainstream" the handicapped and those who want to shelter them, between the camps of the blind and the "low vision people," there is widespread agreement on the need for rehabilitation. Yet I heard the frequent complaint that most ophthalmologists are interested only in cures and treatment. "It's not that we are unsympathetic," one doctor told me. "It's just that we are uncomfortable telling people that we can't fix their problems and that they have to learn to live with them."

I often felt guilty about the blind and wondered—as I had asked Dr. DeFini—if they resent us, the merely half-blind. "In the kingdom of the blind, the one-eyed man is king," says Dr. Faye. But the "kings" are apt to be unpopular. "The blind are very distrustful of the low vision people, whom they regard as a threat," she says. "They don't want to change the definition of blindness; they don't want to admit low vision into their purview. They really only have blindness."

But I have also come across blind people who don't feel that way at all, and they are usually the ones who manage to lead near-normal and highly accomplished lives. They include jurists, businessmen, scientists, writers, athletes—and Josephine DeFini.

Their attitude was well expressed by Winifred Holt in her last public speech in 1945: "We walk and win by faith and not by sight."

10

I sometimes catch myself expecting a cure, although *expecting* is probably too strong a word. It is more an instinct, a mental habit that makes one believe that somehow things will get better.

There is always the lingering hope for some dramatic discovery. We "macular degenerates" rarely meet without asking one another, "Heard anything new?" Both in the press and by word of mouth, reports about new treatments abound. Most of the stories so far have been exaggerated or false and the procedures unproven. Yet their promoters often charge stiff fees. Dubious medications also appear; one recent flurry involved shark cartilage, although experts point out that such cartilage is never formulated the same way twice ("it depends on the shark"). Pricey vitamins are sold under various fancy labels, although they cannot accomplish any more than inexpensive generic brands. Zinc, much publicized at one time, has not proved to be helpful. Researchers have found that people with a lifelong habit of eating leafy green vegetables are less susceptible than others to eye disease, in part because these vegetables contain antioxidants. But it is not clear what other components may be at work, and certainly a sudden switch to a vast intake of greens has not been shown to make any difference.

Some years ago, there was much excitement about thalidomide, which inhibits the growth of new blood vessels. Tragically misused, it caused the birth of thousands of deformed babies in the 1950s and early 1960s, but researchers now thought that with proper application it could prevent the bursting of cells in macular degeneration. So far, it has not worked. Another hope was interferon, a drug also used against cancer. I was one of five hundred patients involved in a year-long test (chaired by David Guyer). Three times a week, I gave myself an injection, which had to be prepared by someone else because I could not see the proper quantity in the syringe. Although the test failed to produce positive results, this trial popularized the concept of drug treatment for age-related macular degeneration. The advantage of drug therapy is that it will avoid laser-induced damage to the retina. Guyer and others are especially excited by the discovery of a chemical called VEGF (vascular endothelial growth factor), believed to cause blood-vessel proliferation. An experimental antibody is being tested in a major trial.

Other drugs, in pill or injection form, are also being tested to see if they can prevent or slow the growth of abnormal blood vessels.

There is also much enthusiasm about photo-dynamic therapy—injecting a dye and activating it by light energy that does not destroy the retina. Highly encouraging tests have shown that the dye can cause selective closure of abnormal blood vessels.

The Scheie Eye Institute in Philadelphia has helped launch a program involving twenty-five centers to explore whether laser therapy can be used preventively. Radiation is also being tried. At the Massachusetts Eye and Ear Infirmary, among other studies, scientists are testing proton beams to reduce cell proliferation. Many institutions are experimenting with surgery. At Duke University and at Johns Hopkins, doctors are attempting to detach and rotate the retina to reposition the macula.

Elsewhere, including at the Harkness Eye Institute at Columbia-Presbyterian, researchers are hoping to transplant healthy cells of the retina to replace damaged ones. Unfortunately, retina transplants are infinitely more complex than cornea transplants. "The good news," Dr. Guyer says, "is that we are now able to surgically perform retinal transplantation and there does not seem to be rejection by the eye of this foreign material. The bad news is that we still have no way to connect the approximately 1.2 million fibers from the retina to the brain." In order to get useful vision, those 1.2 million fibers must be attached from eye to brain in exact order. "It's a nightmare with all the spaghetti there," says Guyer. "But it's no longer science fiction."

Another idea that would have sounded like science fiction until recently is a microchip to replace damaged light receptors in the retina and connect to the brain. An ophthalmologist and his brother, an electrical engineer, are experimenting with such devices in animals, and so far these have worked for brief periods.

There has been much publicity about other interventions, but doctors emphasize that all of these are experimental techniques and that for the majority of patients, surgery is presently still unwise.

My own condition improved unexpectedly at one point, due partly to a cataract operation. (A cataract is a clouding of the eye lens that is unrelated to macular degeneration but often aggravates it.) The procedure, conducted by Dr. Jack Dodick at Manhattan Eye, Ear and Throat Hospital, took a few hours. Dodick quickly made a small incision in my eye. Despite the anesthesia, it was painful for an instant and reminded me of all those ancient operations with bronze lancets or straws. Through the opening, Dodick removed the scarred lens of my eye and slipped in a plastic substitute. This plastic lens was tightly rolled up as the doctor inserted it; then, once in place, it unfolded itself in a way that sounded almost incredible when Dodick described it to me later. After a few weeks, my vision became clearer than it had been, as the new, artificial lens admitted more light. The improvement was also due to what the doctors called a slight "stabilization" of my condition, something that occurs occasionally without any real explanation. My left eye was now back to 20/70. This enabled me to read normal print again—in good light and for short periods. There was no guarantee that this improvement would last, and indeed it has not. As I work on this manuscript, I am back to where I was before.

The emotional effects of macular degeneration often seem more troublesome than the physical ones. I frequently recall Dr. DeFini's summary of these emotional effects and I ask myself to what extent my own feelings coincide with her description. Denial? I think I have mostly overcome that and faced up to my condition, but there are relapses. Besides, the line between denial and heroic effort is hard to draw. I continue to write in the manner I have described, but I would not try to play tennis and I would not want to be near a duck hunter with macular degeneration.

Anger? Depression? Yes. Unable to make out a film on television or to pick out a CD I wanted to play, I have sometimes stomped out of the room in fury. I have been known to hurl a magazine to the floor when, for the thousandth time, I realized that I could not read print without magnification, and I have cursed my various magnifiers as clumsy and inadequate. Still, these gadgets are indispensable and I am furious at myself when I forget to take one along to a restaurant or meeting (a Freud-oriented friend believes that such forgetfulness represents an unconscious protest). I often take notes too hurriedly, so that later I cannot decipher them and I crumple the paper in a rage. Anger, of course, may be displaced from the immediate cause to different targets, and I try hard—not always successfully—not to take out my anger on others. I sometimes indulged in an excessive meal or an extra drink by way of compensation, but they did not seem to help much, either.

As my outward view dimmed, I was inclined to look inward. What I found there often were mental pictures—pictures, for instance, of myself as a child picking wild strawberries on a hot summer day, as a young man flirting with a girl over a dry martini in an exotic bar, as an editor going without sleep for twenty hours to put a magazine to bed. All this gave me a sharp sense of loss. For some, nostalgia provides comfort, but I think of it as a menace. Few things are harder to accept than one's lost youth—except the loss of those one loves. My inner snapshots of nostalgia alternated with inner pictures of mourning for people close to me who had died.

Inevitably, I thought about my own death. I almost found myself envying the ancient Egyptians, who believed that a magic eye could overcome the ultimate darkness (for that matter, I envied all others who believe in an afterlife). I told myself that I was being melodramatic, but macular degeneration is labeled "age-related" for good reason—it is a constant reminder of advancing years. As a journalist and watcher of the American scene, I had always been struck by the extraordinary and paradoxical American attitude toward the old. On the one hand, we try to be cheerful about them and dote on stories about elderly people dancing and falling in love and having sex and enjoying life like everyone else. On the other hand, we assemble them in retirement communities, those voluntary and often quite luxurious enclaves, like orphanages at the other end of life. I knew that to many they are a welcome godsend, but in my imagination they were always surmounted by clouds of forced jollity mixed with emanations of death.

At the same time, the old have acquired huge political power. We seek to ban ageism and institute laws preventing it. But no legal rules can replace the spirit still found in many other societies. There, the experience and even wisdom of the old are prized, without anyone pretending that age does not matter, and where, above all, the old more easily mingle with the young.

These thoughts, however, were theories I formed while I was still young or middle-aged. As I grew older myself, theory gave way to a different kind of understanding. I realized that industrial society inevitably disperses family and separates the generations. Retirement communities and laws against age discrimination are probably the best we can hope for. I also recognize the obvious: No matter what society does to ease the burden, growing old is an experience that each human being must face largely alone.

The experience came to me gradually, in small steps. When I went to a dinner at my club in New York, I often came home grumbling that so many members were so old—until I realized that I was joining them. Women seemed to smile at me with particular warmth, which I found delightful—until I realized they were smiling at a father figure. The contents of my medicine cabinet overflowed and in my address book the section with names and phone numbers of doctors grew longer than the restaurant section. Ticket sellers in movie theaters and at the Washington or Boston shuttle looked at me and not so much asked as announced, "Senior citizen." My mandatory retirement at sixty-five from my job as editor in chief of Time Inc. was painful. I was prepared for it and I had watched innumerable friends and acquaintances making the best of leaving more or less important positions, but I hated it anyway.

All this happened well before macular degeneration set in, but the disease made it worse. I was often less angry about my poor vision than about my aging; there were things I could do to circumvent my visual loss, but there was nothing to be done about the passage of time. I was irritated by any attempt to sentimentalize aging, including Browning's famous, fatuous lines: "Grow old along with me! The best is yet to be . . ."

I saw no redeeming feature in growing old, and I hated the shrinkage of the future. I kept these feelings mostly to myself, but, with her keen antennae, Louise sensed them. "It seems to me that you are depressed and I understand why," she said. "If I was losing my eyesight I would be moaning and bitching and banging my head against the wall."

I sometimes asked friends, "Do I seem different? Do I seem sad?" They usually answered evasively. I finally recognized that Louise was right. As Dr. DeFini pointed out, people who are depressed often don't recognize it. I knew enough about the subject to understand I was not suffering from clinical depression, the kind of paralyzing despair that makes life unbearable. But I did realize that the mixture of fretting about age and the frustration about my loss of vision was changing my personality and my behavior. I lapsed into stretches of gloom and long silences.

Louise urged me to take antidepressants. I resisted because I have always had an aversion to drugs, including sleeping pills, and believed firmly that one must cope with one's own emotions. But I finally gave in and my doctor did suggest a mild dose of medication. My depression gradually lifted, not only thanks to pharmacology. I was cheered by the good reception of my autobiography. In 1996, I wrote an article about my struggle with macular degeneration for *The New Yorker*. The piece provoked a huge response. Hundreds of people wrote that they had relatives or friends with macular degeneration or suffered from the disease themselves. In letter after letter, they confided that they felt less isolated, less lonely, less confused because I had precisely reflected their own experience. As one correspondent put it: "Reading your article, I kept thinking 'Did I write this or did he?'" Another wrote, "I thought I was reading about myself." Still another told me, "One of my friends of 50 years suffered like you of this disease. I am 83 and have been lucky so far, so I was able to read her the article. It was most encouraging to her." Some letter writers offered theories about how or why they had contracted the disease. One Briton attributed it to his World War II service in the western desert, where General Montgomery forbade his troops to wear sunglasses. Another traced the onset to the time when he started washing himself indoors rather than in a brook outside, at the insistence of his "then wife."

A writer in Boston, Marilyn Jurich, sent me excerpts from her forthcoming book of poetry, *The Eye Inside the Storm.* One of the poems is called "Quintet for 4½ Senses": "All of us have our blind spots—yes? / But oh, what strange illuminations / stray through closing spaces." Their letters brought me a sense of fellowship with people I did not know but with whom I shared a burden. I also recognized that this fellowship involved many who were coping with other handicaps and challenges, including the challenges of ordinary life.

One of the more intriguing comments came from my daughter Mandy: "I didn't know ninety percent of what had happened, of what you felt, or your experiences until the article," she said. "How typical of a journalist: Only by writing it did you really tell us about details like the testing card. I knew about the magnifiers and the talking watch, but I thought they were just your latest set of gadgets. You had given me a doctor's report but not a 'what's going on in your life' report."

The support of my friends and family was a comfort, although too much sympathy could actually be dispiriting. Occasional flashes of impatience from Louise ("I've always been impatient and I still am") were actually helpful because they made me feel that I was treated normally and not as an invalid.

Not that my depression was lifted once and for all; it comes rushing back treacherously at certain moments. It might happen when I push the wrong phone number or am unable to find a pair of cuff links or lose sight of a companion during a walk once too often. At a recent large wedding, I made my way back from the dance floor alone and could not find my table. The trivial incident threw me into a black mood. I find that I must be permanently ready to fight back against depression.

11

One way to fight back is through humor. I sometimes joke about all the ugly things I don't have to see anymore. I have no problems with Mr. Magoo and found the recent attempts to suppress a remake of the cartoon quite unjustified.

Another way of fighting back is to treat the situation as a kind of game or contest, trying to outwit stubbornly resistant and illusive objects. This is often merely a matter of touch, and I developed my own version of the strategies I had observed in the Lighthouse rehabilitation class: using my fingers rather than my eyes to guide the razor; feeling the toothbrush before applying the paste, which might otherwise spill all over the sink; counting the buttons on a CD player; asking the restaurant to fax me a menu ahead of time so I won't have to struggle with it while ordering.

All this requires immense patience; macular degeneration is a relentless teacher of that virtue.

I can sign a restaurant check or a credit-card slip with the help of a magnifier, and I can tap out a telephone number because I have memorized the keypad. I've also memorized panels in familiar elevators, like home and office, but in strange buildings, I have a hard time finding the right button. I sometimes crouch or even kneel, with my eye close to the panel, trying to make out the numbers. Once a startled messenger, entering the elevator, found me in this position and asked, "Are you praying we make it to the lobby?" In fact, I sometimes miss the lobby and end up in the basement. Whenever there are others in the car, I will ask them to push the button for me. It is usually not necessary to explain that I have poor eyesight; people seem to expect this from an elderly man, which is a depressing thought.

Yes, I have learned to ask for help, but even small triumphs in difficult situations symbolize a larger truth: that I can still lead an independent life and that knowledge is a tonic. As Dr. DeFini says, "It's never going to be the same, but eventually we learn to live with things and find ways around them."

Dr. Faye has the same message. She recalls her father, a businessman, who had severe macular degeneration for twenty years, but continued to work beyond retirement, until he died close to ninety. "I never saw him blink an eye, literally, over macular degeneration," she says. "He got right into alternatives, had people read to him, even dealt with surveyors' maps." He would say, "I will look at this as a life experience, something I will live with." I certainly have blinked, but I try to behave the same way. There is an almost seductive appeal in the prospect of sinking into despair, in the notion of no longer fighting or having to make special efforts. But it is a treacherous appeal and must be resisted. Even on my more downcast days, I never really let go of the determination not to be defeated by those mysterious leaking cells.

Recently, the Massachusetts Eye and Ear Infirmary asked me to present its annual Reynolds Achievement Awards for people who have overcome the loss of vision, hearing, or speech or have helped others to do so. (The award is named for Dr. Edward Reynolds, cofounder of the infirmary.) The recipients were Bonnie Poitras Tucker, a highly successful deaf lawyer and legal scholar, and Cara Dunne, a blind championship skier and cyclist. The indomitable and cheerful spirit they displayed in surmounting their disabilities was deeply moving and caused me to think a great deal about the "handicapped."

I had always considered them as a group apart. It was not easy for me to accept that I was one of them. The label is often vague, the category ill-defined. But it is all too real, and how we cope with it says a great deal about ourselves and our society. We have become very careful not to offend anybody and have even introduced a new, euphemistic, and often silly vocabulary—"mobility deficient" and "mentally challenged." The intent is praiseworthy, but tinkering with language will hardly change people's attitudes. Those of us who are dealing with infirmity need to have a reasonably thick skin.

No country in history has taken so much care to protect and help the disabled as the United States, from mandating special access ramps for wheelchairs to legislation against discrimination in employment. We insist, like the Lighthouse, that the handicapped should lead normal lives, or as close to normal as possible. In fact, we sometimes seem to command them to do so. We believe that obstacles are there to be overcome. We tend to regard such overcoming almost as a military campaign or a sporting feat. This can be pushed too far. As Bonnie Tucker points out, not every deaf person can be, or wants to be, a lawyer. Not every blind person can be, or wants to be, an athlete. But those who, like Bonnie Poitras Tucker and Cara Dunne, do achieve extraordinary goals can inspire others to reach for lesser but equally important feats, whether merely reading a book in braille or jogging through the park. Cara Dunne, who lost her eyes to cancer when she was a child, refused to accept her limitations. Not long ago, she told one of her doctors, "If you offered me sight right now, I would tell you to give it to someone who felt it was something they could not live without. . . . I don't think the things I need to be able to do are things that can't be done without sight."

This attitude represents a very American refusal to bow to what in other civilizations and in other times was regarded as fate. Yet fate is precisely what I have increasingly thought about since the onset of my disease, and I have learned a new humility toward it.

We generally want perfection—perfect health, perfect sight. We are reluctant to settle for less. I have come to realize that few of us are entirely without handicaps and that there are many disabilities that may not require wheelchairs or reading machines. We resist the idea that damage is not the exception but the rule, part of the tissue of life. But once we accept this, life itself begins to look different. It looks more difficult, more complex, but also more rewarding. We appreciate—or should—not what is missing but what is left. Frustrated as I am by what I cannot see, I revel in what I can see.

One of my children asked me, "Don't you rail against what happened to you? Don't you ever demand, 'Why me?'" I do not ask that question. Why things happen to some people and not to others is the ultimate mystery. Many see it as part of God's inscrutable plan, and many see it as the absurd randomness of existence. I would like to believe in the first version, but I am more persuaded by the second. Either way, my own attitude is acceptance without resignation.

During one of our conversations about our disease, Nick Stevenson said, "This doesn't close the book of life. To restore our emotional balance, we have only to put our hands over our eyes." As he told me this, he did, in fact, place both hands over his eyes. He was saying, of course, that total loss of sight is so much worse than our limited vision.

I find so much left to me that to complain almost seems sacrilegious. So many others have so much less. This notion that things could be worse—my old mantra and the ultimate way of fighting back—remains entirely true. But in the end, it is not enough. One cannot measure one's life in comparison to that of others, whether they are worse off or better off. That leads either to smugness or envy. One must measure and conduct one's life on its own terms, for the pain or pleasure, the failures or achievements, within one's own being. I want to be able to say not that "things could be worse" but that "things are good." They are—most of the time.

Struggling for sight has given me a sense of being part of a timeless story. I feel an odd kinship with the Greeks trembling before Athena's withering glance, with Odin exchanging an eye for wisdom, with the magician-doctors offering potions and incantations, and with those single-cell organisms, their eyespots turning toward the light.

I tell myself being half-blind is not a bad metaphor for the human condition.

SELECTED BIBLIOGRAPHY

Albert, Daniel M., and Diane D. Edwards. *History of Ophthalmology.* Blackwell Science, 1996.

Berthier, Louis Alex. *Memoir of the Campaigns of General Bonaparte in Egypt and Syria, and the Operations of General Desaix in Upper Egypt.* Translated by Thomas Evanson White. J. S. Barr, London, 1805.

Bloodgood, Edith Holt, ed., in collab. with Rufus Graves Mather. *First Lady of the Lighthouse.* The Lighthouse, 1952.

Burgin, Richard. *Conversations with Jorge Luis Borges.* Holt, Rinehart and Winston, 1968.

Cotterell, Arthur. *The Encyclopedia of Mythology.* Anness Publishing Limited, 1996.

Cross, Warren D., and Lawrence Lynn. *Your Vision.* MasterMedia Limited, 1994.

Selected Bibliography

Eden, John, ed. *The Physician's Guide to Cataracts, Glaucoma, and Other Eye Problems.* Consumer Reports Books, 1992.

Eliade, Mircea, ed. *Encyclopedia of Religion.* MacMillan, 1987.

Fensch, Thomas, ed. *Conversations with James Thurber.* University Press of Mississippi, 1989.

Huxley, Aldous. *The Art of Seeing.* Creative Arts Books, 1942.

Schatz, Howard, H. Richard McDonald, and Robert N. Johnson. *For My Patient: Macular Degeneration.* Retina Research Fund, 1993.

Seiderman, Arthur S., and Steven E. Marcus. *20/20 Is Not Enough: The New World of Vision.* Alfred A. Knopf, 1989.

Thurber, James. *Selected Letters of James Thurber.* University Press of Mississippi, 1989.

A NOTE ABOUT THE AUTHOR

Henry Grunwald was the editor in chief of *Time* magazine and all other Time Inc. publications. He served as the U.S. ambassador to Austria and is the author of *One Man's America: A Journalist's Search for the Heart of His Country*. He lives in New York City with his wife, Louise, and their Australian terrier, Harry.

A NOTE ON THE TYPE

This book was set in Adobe Garamond. Designed for the Adobe Corporation by Robert Slimbach, the fonts are based on types first cut by Claude Garamond (c. 1480–1561). Garamond was a pupil of Geoffroy Tory and is believed to have followed the Venetian models, although he introduced a number of important differences, and it is to him that we owe the letter we now know as "old style." He gave to his letters a certain elegance and feeling of movement that won their creator an immediate reputation and the patronage of Francis I of France.

Composed by Dix Type,
Syracuse, New York

Printed and bound by Quebecor Fairfield,
Fairfield, Pennsylvania

Designed by Dorothy S. Baker